VERY NICE WORK IF YOU CAN GET IT

VERY
NICE WORK
IF YOU CAN GET IT

VERY NICE WORK IF YOU CAN GET IT

The Socially Useful Production Debate

Edited by
Collective Design/Projects

Contributions from
Cliff Allum
Erica Carter
Cynthia Cockburn
Philip Cooke
Mike Cooley
Paul Field
Ursula Huws
Chris Lee
Sonia Liff
John Lovering
Brian Lowe
Vin McCabe
Seymour Melman
David Noble
David Pelly
Hilary Wainwright

SPOKESMAN

First published in 1985 by:
Spokesman
Bertrand Russell House
Gamble Street
Nottingham
England
Tel. 0602 708318
Copyright © Spokesman, 1985

This book is copyright under the Berne Convention. All rights are reserved. Apart from any fair dealing for the purpose of private study, research, criticism or review, as permitted under the Copyright Act, 1956, no part of this publication may be reproduced, stored in a retrieval system, or transmitted, in any form or by any means, electronic, electrical, chemical, mechanical, photocopying, recording or otherwise, without the prior permission of the copyright owner. Enquiries should be addressed to the publisers.

British Library Cataloguing in Publication Data

Very nice work if you can get it: the socially useful production dabate.
 1. Labor economics
 I. Collective design
 331   HD4901

ISBN 0-85124-430-0
ISBN 0-85124-431-9 Pbk

Typeset, printed and bound by the Russell Press Ltd., Nottingham.
(Tel. 0602 784505).

Contents

Foreword by Audrey Wise	7
Preface and Acknowledgements	12
Introduction	13

PART I: Workers Plans: From Products to Popular Planning

1. After the Lucas Plan — *Mike Cooley* — 19
2. Sheffield City Council Employment Department — 27
3. Popular Planning and the GLC — *Hilary Wainwright* — 37
4. Making People Powerful: Coventry Workshop — *Paul Field* — 53
5. A Report from the Unit for the Development of Alternative Products — *Brian Lowe* — 61

PART II: Extending the Politics

6. Not my Type — Choices in Technology and Organisation for Printing — *Cynthia Cockburn* — 74
7. Worker Co-operatives in Wales: A Framework for Socially Useful Production? — *Philip Cooke* — 86
8. Production for Development — Alternatives from the Third World — *Chris Lee* — 95
9. Arms Conversion and the Labour Movement — *David Pelly* — 104
10. Arms Conversion: A View from the USA — *Seymour Melman* — 120
11. Socially Useful Production and Local Strategies — *John Lovering* — 126

PART III: Looking to the Future

12. Present Tense Technology — *David Noble* — 139
13. Challenging Commoditisation — Producing Usefulness outside the Factory — *Ursula Huws* — 149
14. Socially Useful Production and the Unemployed — *Cliff Allum & Vin McCabe* — 168
15. Women Factory Workers — What Could Socially Useful Production Mean for Them? — *Sonia Liff* — 178
16. Alternative Products in West Berlin: Mehringhof, Netzwerk and Goldrausch — *Erica Carter* — 187

Conclusion — 199

Resources & Bibliography — 209

Contributors — 213

Foreword
Audrey Wise

I was brought up on the notion that socialism is about "production for use, not private profit". It seemed a good idea, but gradually became less vivid and more vague to me: until the Lucas Workers' Plan, of which I am an enthusiastic advocate.

In the intervening years, however, most socialists — and certainly the Labour Party — seemed to become wedded to the idea that "the state" means "the public" and "the public" means "people", therefore "the state" equals "the people". So nationalisation replaced common ownership as a goal, state intervention became a god in itself, and we ultimately wound up with the National Enterprise Board. This rationalised quite a lot of employment down the drain with the justification that it was saving some jobs and they probably would *all* have gone without the NEB. I asked Leslie Murphy, its head, if the NEB sought for (or even would accept) advice, suggestions and information from Shop Stewards' Committees. He said "No. The NEB worked by appointing, then monitoring, managements who would be sacked if they proved incompetent". To which I replied that a good many people would have lost their jobs on the road to that proof.

I became disenchanted with the idea that "state intervention" tells very much about what is actually on offer. I observed that the Portuguese dictatorship had nationalised banks. I started to substitute a series of questions by which to evaluate policies: *Who benefits? Who decides? Who pays? Who suffers? and will people in general have more control over their own lives?*

It seems to me that this important book on Socially Useful Production is about how to answer those questions. Its essence is an insistence that production must be re-defined to include services as well as goods, and that "socially useful" applies to the methods and relations of production as well as to the product.

The view that all wealth derives from manufacturing is widely held, as much on the left as on the right. Here that view is challenged. Socially useful production is partly about manufactured products, but also about all the other uses of labour. A physiotherapist massaging a limb is at least as productive as an aspirin maker. Why is economic growth only thought to include things which enter the market; and economically active defined only as having paid work? The potatoes we grow in our garden are not classed as part of economic growth, but when we eat them we think they are. Furthermore, we know they haven't been poisoned in the growing method. They are under our control. The woman producing a pie at home is not economically active, but the same woman producing a pie in a factory is! Thank goodness this is shown to be nonsense. How can we improve the economy if we cannot even describe it? If we tie our definitions to the present system, then we keep our solutions also within that system and do not move towards transforming it.

The whole Labour movement approves of public spending. But too often discussion centres on the level of public spending rather than its nature. How that spending is allocated, by whom, and using what criteria, is as crucial as the level.

The last Labour Government spent massively on trying to stem the rising unemployment. It poured money into companies, especially big ones, by way of grants, subsidies and allowances. These came from the Treasury, the Department of Industry, and the Department of Employment, and were mostly unaccountable. But unemployment grew.

A recurrent theme here is closeness to individuals and to small groups, and the importance of local action and the local economy. In total contrast there is the Tories' method which purports to help employment in the worst hit areas by removing protection from workers and giving concessions to employers. The method advocated here is the analysis of local needs and then trying to meet those needs in and by a local community. This is equally different from the orthodox Labour policy of giving inducements to big companies to relocate.

The pervasive Tory myth is Tina. There Is No Alternative. "People are unemployed because they do not make what people want to buy, or they do not produce the right goods at the right price". It must soon dawn on people that this is a myth. People want all kinds of goods and services, but whether they can afford to buy them bears no relationship to the extent of their need. For example, surely sooner or later the simple truth that people need homes yet building workers are unemployed will take hold of people's minds, and that kind of realisation will help towards the election of a Labour Government. But will the Labour Government then act on those simple truths? Or will it founder on the old rocks?

Previous Labour Governments have tried to relate to workers as takers of wages, and influence them towards wage restraint to avoid inflation. But taking wages is at the end of the productive process and is not the deciding factor in it. There is a sense in which arguments both for and against wage restraint are equally irrelevant if the economy is collapsing, for no policy can ensure improved living standards then. A Labour Government needs to build relationships with workers as producers of goods and services, to enable them to use their skills and knowledge of their own needs as workers and consumers, to build on their inescapable commitment. For bosses move their money around whereas workers invest their lifetimes. Instead, up to now workers have been driven to the conclusion that political action has failed them. They then became easy prey for Tory ideology.

We have to ensure that this does not happen again. The next Labour Government must not go the way of the French Socialist Government — so often quoted by Mrs Thatcher as evidence that There is No Alternative, everyone adopts Tory policies in the end.

No doubt different people will get different things from *Very Nice Work*, emphasising different aspects of the problem. I see it as an exploration of ideas which the Labour movement needs if it is to undo Tory damage. However, this does not start with the next General Election, and must not wait for it. It would be a disservice to the book to imply that it is only about the future. In any case, the future always starts now. This is very much about the present, about the initiatives being taken now, not least by certain Labour Councils but also by many other people.

People should not be misled into believing that they must wait for politicians before they act or before they try to build. The achievement of the Mondragon co-operative complex in Franco Spain, and the case studies in this book, are evidence of possibilities in unfavourable circumstances. However, there can be no doubt that good political help (as from the GLC) can be of immense value. Any scrap of power which can be used and any resources which can be tapped should be put at the service of those trying to find new ways of working, and new ways of intervening in the economy and in their environment.

This book is stimulating and informative. Its ideas may help us towards a Socially Useful Government.

A nineteenth century utopia

THREE UTOPIAS

1. Robert Owen is perhaps one of the best known radical paternalists. His most successful project was his first enterprise — a spinning mill in New Lanark. What he set out to do, in common with other utopians of the time, was to reform the excesses of C19th industrial capitalism. His results were, within limitations, progressive. The mills were turned into model factories with working conditions, equipment, hours and wages better than those found in contemporary industry. Accommodation, elementary schooling and a creche were provided (claimed as the first in Britain). As a business it was profitable. From the experience of the mills Owen decided to set up a self-supporting community. In the first instance he did this on a small scale. He then implemented a 'grand' scheme in 1825 by buying a village, New Harmony, in Indiana (USA). The idealism and limited material capacity for self-sufficiency did not take long to fail. In spite of this and his off-beam morality, Owen continued to follow a radical path, especially in the area of trade union development.

2. Prince Kropotkin was a contemporary of William Morris, and his ideas vied with socialism for popular support in the mid-1880s. Both had an influence upon and were influenced by the development of ideas in the United States. The "New World" was in many ways viewed as the "land of the free", as space, as untrammelled nature and, as Owen's venture suggests, an ideal location to establish utopias and "alternative communities". Kropotkin advocated a particular relation between industry, agriculture and community, which was based on networks of small scale producers. These were founded on farms, small industry and industrial villages. In this context he had a view of socially useful production which centred on a community meeting its needs and supporting itself, and at the same time extending labour as social labour. Work was projected as something spanning manual and mental activity under the direct control of workers. These ideas have been influential and inspired many early planners ideas.

3. Perkins Gilman was an American woman writing at the turn of the century and after. She was mainly concerned with the consequences of capitalism (industrialisation and urbanisation) as it affected women. She argued (*Women and Economics*, 1898) that the domestic subordination of women to housework/motherhood was blocking the development of society as a whole. In addition, she stated that collective domestic life was important in the development of socialism. At the core of her project was a belief in the inseparability of socialism and feminism.

Gilman posed her ideas of a new domestic order around notions of the kitchenless home. She advocated eating in social centres which, besides dining facilities, would include lounges, libraries, baths, gymnasia, playrooms, etc. Private space was retained but 'free association' in public was to have a much higher profile.

Preface

Without the support of the West Midlands County Council's Economic Development Committee this book would not have been possible. Besides funding much of the work on it, and giving initial backing to the co-op, within their co-operative development policy, they have supported several of the book's contributors. These are: Coventry Trades Council Unemployed Workers Project; Coventry Workshop; and The Unit for the Development of Alternative Products.

Over the period of the rise of the Labour dominated Metropolitan Councils we have seen the kind of opening up of the cultural and economic space in which socially useful production can develop. Such progress is, though, in real danger of being killed off before the end of its infancy. The massive onslaught against local government in general and the Mets in particular has effect not only within the political structures of the local state. Cuts are made and power, space, wellbeing and freedoms are lost across a very broad band of society. So, while this action clearly damages the growth rate of a politics of socially useful production, what this book will show is that this type of politics is not that easy to contain. It cannot be abolished.

We would like to thank Mandy Root for valuable insights into our project. Thanks also to Roger Dicker of West Midlands County Council for forbearance and humour. Mary Ballard's rapid service has been much appreciated. Our gratitude is also expressed to all contributors and to Spokesman for recognising the merits of this undertaking.

This book has been edited by the founding members of Collective Design/Midland: Tony Fry, Philippa Goodall, Michael Green, Derrick Price and Paul Willis. Collective Design/Midland was, until recently, a worker co-operative in Coventry. At the time of writing it has divided into two parts spanning graphic production (still a Coventry co-op) and research, exhibition and publications (now a Birmingham based group). Both are looking for and helping to create a new relation between design and the left.

Collective Design/Projects 1985

Introduction

This book is about Socially Useful Production. Yet we have to start from the fact that there is no single object, movement or project which completely contains and delimits the term.

Much of industrial history over the past two hundred years can be read as an account of demands for socially useful production. Demands that led to a struggle over what is produced, by whom, under what conditions, through what technical means. Demands that put questions about who profited, who starved; about how classes gained and sustained power while others were oppressed. A full history of Socially Useful Production would be linked at every point with a history of the development and growth of capitalism, and the struggle for socialist alternatives. Nevertheless, we mention a few particular moments in such a history in the first of the 'boxes' which, all the way through the book, draw attention to issues and reading for which there was no space in the main text.

Exploring the meanings of Socially Useful Production is a major objective of this book. The task is undertaken in the context of a widespread pursuit of alternatives to the enormous, inflicted, social hardship of the 1980s. Our concern here is not so much with broad political ideas as with political actions, strategies and structures. In the most general terms, what is being focused upon is a shift from exchange value to use value. In other words, the movement away from production with the aim of maximising profit, towards production for social use and need. Such a view does not presume needs to be uniform. We recognise that it varies according to who you are, what you are and circumstances. Also, that we can, and should, debate and argue about what *is* needed, all the time.

The centrality of Socially Useful Production in its most open sense renders it slippery and vague. Everyone on the Left is in favour of it — in a 'general' sort of way — but it is inserted into political agendas at many different points and in many different guises.

In Britain during the last 20 years it has been identified with the efforts of trade unionists to stave off redundancy, not by piecemeal action, but by drawing up plans which would maintain the profitability of their companies, while converting them to the production of useful commodities. Such plans (of which the most famous is the report of the Shop Stewards Combine at Lucas Aerospace, discussed early in the book) also proposed ways in which new technologies could be employed to enrich and develop workers' lives instead of leading to massive unemployment and the deskilling of those lucky enough to keep their jobs.

Of course there have been, are, will be, many other starting-points, from quite other places. For instance, a concern about the damage done to the earth, to animals, to the environment: the 'greening' of recent political movements. For instance, a realisation in parts of the 'Third World' that the 'developed countries' and transnational corporations and agencies had their own uses to which to put the process of 'development'. For instance, a knowledge of the structural place held by arms production, on an ever greater scale, in the industrial production of the major powers: swords to plowshares, missiles (and the jobs at stake in missiles) into what? Nor have issues of planning and purpose only been raised by unions in industrial production — public service unions have explored the benefits and the social relations of different forms of transport systems, health provision, housing.

Notice, too, that the debate about Socially Useful Production can encompass different stages of the production process: forms of ownership and control; work practices, labour processes, job satisfaction, challenge, involvement; useful products; and, all the time, questions about where and what 'production' is, to which the later essays in this book insistently return. These themes recur throughout this book, but they are not simply stated and celebrated. Socially Useful Production is also subjected to criticism both as a general term and in its practical application within particular projects.

We have collected these essays in order to explore a number of questions about Socially Useful Production in a constructive way; to describe some of the projects planned or in existence, and to help provide a political agenda which is open to the concerns of Socially Useful Production. To this end we need to ask what is important about this form of production.

The central idea of Socially Useful Production is, in its simplest formulation, that we should collectively produce those things that we need, rather than things that are frivolous, dangerous or even deadly. This is so simple, so 'obvious' an idea that it takes a conscious effort to remind ourselves that the system under which we presently produce and consume goods is predicated on quite different principles. The rationale of capitalism is the production not of commodities and services, but of profits; and the only measure of a thing's worth is its ability to generate profit. This, as we all know, means that those needs backed by purchasing power are met, while those needs for which there is no 'economic' demand go partially or totally unfulfilled. At its most grotesque this 'logic' allows for the creation of a steady supply of cruise missiles, but for a shortfall of kidney machines. A central demand of Socially Useful Production is that we challenge the logic which underpins such decisions.

But the question of what commodities are produced is locked into other, equally important questions. Capitalism, in its search for profits, not only makes amoral decisions about *what* should be produced, it also translates as many human needs as possible into commodities which can be bought and sold. Our needs for emotional and sexual life; for respect, for pleasure, autonomy, stimulation and so on, are returned to us as a need for this or that commodity. Hence, capitalism's great triumph has been the creation and stable supply of an extraordinary number of commodities. This is, in its own way, often exciting and attractive. Many commodities fill pre-existing needs and others open up potential new sources of creativity and pleasure for those who can afford them. But before we become too excited by the idea of capitalism as an Aladdin's cave, we need to consider what we have lost, given away and had stolen from us in the service of its creation.

It seems clear that one determining principle of production and consumption under capitalism is that a complex and integrated cluster of human needs has been fractured and re-organised into many different social, economic and institutional spheres. For example, we consume as individuals or in families, but we also consume collectively. We need a saucepan or a book, but we also need homes, schools, hospitals, and appropriate forms of transport. Collective consumption of this kind should reflect collective needs, but is constantly returned to us as an individual need, which we can buy like a new saucepan and do without if we cannot afford it. The production of commodities privatises our experience, then, but we should also notice that commodities are not simple and neutral answers to needs. Designed into commodities are the conditions under which they can be consumed, which structure their use and structure their users. For this reason commodities which promise us liberation frequently turn out to lock us into limiting or alienated ways of life.

This book can be read in different orders and used in different ways — but we should indicate its general shape. The early essays evoke and explore the Lucas story, and illustrate a variety of initiatives inside Britain today where similar themes are being pursued in policy experiments. The frame is broadened to make contrasts and connections with work elsewhere: in Wales, which is not England; in Europe; in the Third World, where we look at a case study. There are then two essays on problems of arms conversion: a view from the USA, and one from Britain. Later essays put a series of constructive but also dissenting questions to the whole idea of Socially Useful Production, and start to move the agenda on to further issues which are largely propositional in character. Part Three closes by returning concretely to the present with an experiment in West Berlin. There is a sectin on resources, and a set of suggestions for further reading.

But 'further reading' is not what the authors mainly had in mind! The book is published as the Metropolitan County Councils look set to be abolished, and with them the actual and potential structure for much work of this kind. Where, in the next year or two, will these ideas be debated, by whom, with what effects? We hope the book might help in getting discussions going, of various sorts, in various political contexts. Such is the intended social usefulness of *this* production, and of an exhibition which accompanies it.

PART ONE

Workers' Plans: From Products to Popular Planning

LUCAS THE COMBINE AND THE PLAN

The Lucas Shop Stewards' Combine Committee was formed in 1969 as a response to the Government's re-organisation of the British Aerospace industry. Its initial aims centred on the fight against mass redundancies. By 1973 all thirteen Lucas Aerospace factory sites had affiliated. During 1975-76 the strategy which won the Combine international acclaim was established. This was the creation of a workers' alternative plan. At its core were ideas drawn from the shopfloor via a detailed questionnaire. It was founded on the basic premise that jobs could be saved and more could be created by Lucas moving into new products and markets. In addition, the plan carried the idea of the market being more than the location of a point of economic exchange. Rather, it was seen as populated by people with particular needs for things like cheap transport, low cost energy and better technological support for the disabled. The plan not only registered social and use value through its proposed products, but was also an affirmative statement of the knowledge, creativity and skills of the workers. All these elements gave weight to its political use and acknowledgement in the struggle within and beyond Lucas.

A key feature of the combine organisation was its multi-union, multi-site linking. This made it different and more appropriate to contesting the power of a multinational corporation than conventional trade union structures. When engaged on an alternative plan, such a structure has been viewed as a new form of trade unionism.

Hilary Wainwright and Dave Elliot, *The Lucas Plan*, Allison and Busby, 1982.

CHAPTER ONE

After the Lucas Plan
Mike Cooley

On the front page of the now famous Lucas Workers' plan for Socially Useful Production there is the statement that "there cannot be islands of social responsibility in a sea of depravity". Lucas workers themselves never believed that it would be possible to establish in Lucas Aerospace alone the right to produce socially useful products. Only some of their baton wavers seemed to believe that, or those who sought to decry their activities by suggesting it was Utopian.

The Lucas Plan

What the Lucas workers sought to do was to embark upon an exemplary project which would inflame the imagination of those elsewhere. To do so they recognised that it was necessary to demonstrate in a very practical and direct way the creative power of 'ordinary people'. Further they had to do so in such a fashion as to confirm to 'ordinary people' that they too had the capacity to change their situation; to realise that they are not the objects of history but rather the subjects, capable of building their own futures.

The Lucas workers could see about them the grotesque absurdities of modern industrial society. They were aware of the growing powerlessness and frustration of masses of people as decisions were concentrated in the hands of vast multinational corporations whose size and activities dwarfed that of nation states. It was a courageous attempt to repossess that precious ground of decision making which planners, managers, co-ordinators were removing from them. They highlighted and built upon four major contradictions in industrial society, in the following way.

First, there is the appalling gap which now exists between that which technology could provide for society, and that which it actually does provide. We have a level of technological sophistication such that we can design and produce Concorde, yet in the same society we cannot provide enough simple heating systems to protect old age pensioners from hypothermia. In the winter of 1975-6, 980 died of the cold in the London area alone.

We have senior automotive engineers who sit in front of computerised visual display units 'working interactively to optimise the configuration' of car bodies to make them aerodynamically stable at 120 miles an hour when the average speed of traffic through New York is 6.2 miles an hour. It was in fact 11 miles per hour at the turn of the century when the vehicles were horsedrawn. We find the linear drive forward of complex esoteric technology in the interests of the multinational corporations, and the growing deprivation of communities and the mass of people as a whole.

The second contradiction is the tragic wastage our society makes of its most precious asset — that is the skill, ingenuity, energy, creativity and enthusiasm of its ordinary people. We now have in Britain vast numbers out of work. There are thousands of engineers suffering the degradation of unemployment when we urgently need cheap, effective and safe transport systems for our cities. We have building workers out of a job when by the government's own statistics it is admitted that about seven million people live in semi-slums in this country.

The third contradiction is the myth that computerisation, automation and the use of robotic devices will automatically free human beings from soul destroying backbreaking tasks and leave them free to engage in more creative work. The perception of trade union colleagues and that of millions of workers in the industrial nations is that in most instances the reverse is actually the case. At an individual level, the totality that is a human being is ruthlessly torn apart and its component parts set one against the other. The individual as producer is required to perform grotesque alienated tasks to produce throwaway products to exploit the individual as consumer.

Fourth, there is the growing hostility of society at large to science and technology as at present practised. There seems to be no understanding of the manner in which scientists and technologists are used as mere messenger boys of the multinational corporations whose sole concern is the maximisation of profits. Some people act as though you specified that rust should be sprayed on car bodies before the paint is applied; that all commodities should be enclosed in non recycleable containers, and that every large scale plant you design is produced specifically to pollute the air and the rivers. It is therefore not surprising that some of our most able and sensitive sixth formers will not now study science and technology because they perceive it to be such a dehumanised activity in our society.

Propelled by the frantic linear drive forward of this form of science and technology, we witness the growth of massive structural unemployment. Predictions of 20 million jobless in the EEC countries by 1990 no longer seem absurd.

Lucas Workers and Power

Having identified these contradictions Lucas workers set out to do something about them. They made an audit of their own skills and abilities. They went out to different factories and workshops, and analysed and assessed the production equipment, product ranges and skills at each location. This represented an enormous extension of consciousness, since we are all of us conditioned to view the world through the one lathe we operate or the one desk from which we function. Never are we encouraged or allowed to take a panoramic view of our industry and see how that locates into a wider pattern of society.

Lucas workers then asked their own workmates what they thought they could and should make. In gathering these ideas they did not insist that those with proposals wrote a great thesis about them. They did not make the typical European mistake of confusing linguistic ability with intelligence. They realised that industrial workers expressed their intelligence by what they do and how they organise to do it. If therefore the workers wished to make models of the products, make sketches of them, or build prototypes then that was not only accepted but positively encouraged. Between them they produced some 150 proposals for products which they could make as an alternative to the degradation of unemployment.

Prototypes of these products were built and displayed on a widespread scale. Lucas workers went to the then Labour government and pointed out that its manifesto had said that it stood for 'an irreversible shift of power in the interest of working people'. But the government and in particular the Department of Industry was clearly bewildered by the notion that one might think of products for their use value rather than their exchange value. In addition, trade union bureaucracies — with two exceptions — bitterly resented a rank and file activism which they perceived as a challenge to their leadership. The notion that leadership might be catalytic, enabling and supportive was beyond them.

The whole exercise demonstrated in a very direct way to the

Lucas workers the nature of power relationships. For example, when they proposed the manufacture of heat pumps using natural gas in internal combustion engines the company turned the proposal down saying that it would not be profitable and was incompatible with their product range. Burnley workers subsequently revealed that the company had had a report prepared for them by American Consultants showing that the market for the heat pump would be some thousand million pounds in the private and industrial sectors in the EEC countries, by the late 1980s. Lucas would be willing to forego a market of that kind to demonstrate that it, and it alone, would decide what was made, how it was made, and in whose interest it was made. Lucas workers then quickly recognised that they were dealing not just with an economic system but also a political system concerned with the retention of power.

When the company moved on to the offensive and victimised some of the leading stewards amid world-wide protest there was inadequate support from union leaderships. The Lucas Plan was turned down by the Labour government and rejected by trade unions with the exception of the TGWU and some peripheral support from ASTMS. Lucas workers then felt that the key strategic position was to diffuse the ideas as widely as possible through the Labour and trade union movement. They formed a joint forum of combines and produced a number of very well worthwhile reports. But increasingly they also entered into discussions with those who were contesting election in local government. The Labour Party in London actually wrote into its manifesto that it would seek to restructure industry on the lines of the Lucas Workers' Plan.

After Lucas: the Greater London Council

One of the outcomes which exemplifies this sort of thinking is the Industry and Employment Policy of the Greater London Council. Several instruments were established to implement manifesto commitments. A Popular Planning Unit was established to mobilise masses of people to begin to solve these problems themselves. That was very much in the tradition of the Lucas activity. The Greater London Enterprise Board became a legal entity in November 1982 and began to function as an organisation from February 1983. It was provided with £32m to provide support for sectors of industry and to help in its restructuring. Apart from providing financial assistance in setting up new companies and restructuring old ones, divisions were established to deal with changing power relationships in industry. The Structural Division involves trade union groups in drawing up enterprise plans. At County Hall an Industrial Development Unit has established an early warning system and seeks to involve trade unionists in looking in an active way at the development of their companies.

One of the most innovative steps taken was to establish through the Greater London Enterprise Board a series of Technology Networks throughout London. This is an attempt to build upon the ideas established by the Lucas workers when they had set up the Centre for Alternative Industrial and Technological Systems (CAITS). London has one of the richest seams of higher educational capability to be found any place in the world, with seven polytechnics and three universities. Frequently those in these institutions would like to be involved in solving problems for the communities in which they live, yet the nature of higher education is such that they normally work on either isolated projects or ones which relate to the more long term requirements of the multinational corporations and the 'military-industrial complex'.

By contrast the Technology networks are an attempt to make creative links between the skill and ingenuity of ordinary people and the facilities and knowledge of polytechnics and universities. Three of these networks are geographically based and cover catchment areas of London, whilst two are product based: an Energy network and a New Technology network. Each network will have one or possibly two buildings located close to a university or polytechnic but not normally on the campus. In this way it is possible for the community and academics to meet as it were on neutral ground. Universities can be extremely alienating for the unemployed, for womens' groups, for marginal groups — and possibly for the students, but then they don't have much choice! By having a separate network which is formed into a company and run by a management committee with representatives from the community, trade unions, academic life, special interest groups such as tenants' associations it is possible to provide an environment of 'free access'. This builds upon the idea developed firstly by CAITS but also extends the notion of 'science shops' in Holland and the 'Innovation' Zentrum in West Germany. The idea throughout is to bring science and technology to the community. Thus the Energy network will have mobile units with basic instrumentation which can travel and involve the community in measuring energy losses in its own buildings. Work for the disabled is a linked priority. The disabled throughout London have identified some 450 products and services which they require.

Technology Networks

The New Technology network is working with a variety of groups to develop exciting projects which use advanced technology in a 'human-enhancing way'. They are in conjunction with the University of Manchester Institute of Science and Technology developing a lathe which will enhance human intelligence rather than diminish it. This is a positive response to a tendency towards de-skilling through numerically controlled machine tool systems — it was recently suggested in the United States that the 'ideal worker would have a mental age of 12'. The system worked upon will build upon human knowledge so that it will be possible to allocate to the human being the qualitative subjective elements and to the machine the quantitative elements. Thus the human being will control the machine rather than the other way round.

In advanced expert systems work is in progress with a major medical school to draw on the knowledge of medical consultants and produce rule-based expert systems. However instead of concentrating the knowledge in the hands of a small elite of specialists this expert system will be used to diffuse the knowledge back into general practice and the community. This will mean that the patient in an acute state will not have to be referred to some alienating hospital in the centre of London but can rather be treated in her/his own environment by his/her own general practitioner. The system is so designed that the medical practitioner and the patient can sit in front of a visual display unit (VDU) together and in a democratic fashion review the alternative forms of treatment which may be open and the potential consequences of these.

The New Technology network is also working on the software for a 'product bank'. Each of the networks and a whole range of community groups are feeding in product proposals. Some of these will simply be at the conceptual stage, others will have been taken to prototype stage or even short batch production. If a group of workers wish to set up a co-operative or are looking for alternative products as their company runs into structural difficulty it will be possible to input the type of skills they have got, the facilities they have available and the approximate value of the products they would like to produce. The database will then suggest a number of product options.

Each of the Technology Network buildings will have approximately 8,000 sq ft of workshop space and some 2,000 sq ft of office space, with four or five technologists specially chosen to be able to demystify science and technology and relate to people's practical experience and knowledge. Within the workshop there will be a variety of machine tools and equipment on which prototypes can be built and developed. Facilities will also be available to take these to short batch production before the group involved move out into self-sustaining units. Some of the workshops are going to provide specialist electronic facilities for women. Away from the pressure of male colleagues. Workshops will also develop skills and abilities — in particular diagnostic skills, in an environment which relates to a real world situation, rather than some of the artificially contrived ones at present being operated under the guise of 'training'. The idea will be at all times to develop the full potential of the human being and to provide an educational environment. You programme a robot, you train a dog, but you provide an educational environment for human beings!

The Technology Networks will provide a powerful resource for the people of London. The GLC through GLEB is providing some £4m to support the first five of these in the present year. A Transport network is at an advanced stage of planning. In parallel with this the Information Division of GLEB is producing a whole range of educational material which will be in written and audio-visual form. A number of video films are in the course of preparation. The other divisions of GLEB have between February and November 1983 set up or assisted some 81 companies or projects and created or saved approximately 1,500 jobs.

This is but small compared with the scale and nature of the problems that now confront London, but as with the Lucas Workers' Plan it will provide a powerful exemplary model. Similar exciting projects are afoot in Sheffield, the West Midlands and elsewhere. They are indicating realistic, commonsensical and exciting alternatives to the grotesqueness of monetarism. It is precisely because they are so doing that the Thatcher government is now determined to destroy them. The abilities of these councils to resist will depend largely on the extent of which they involve the community in solving the problems around them. The system of monetarism is incapable of providing answers to these growing structural problems. Projections that in the late 1980s there may be five to six million out of work in the United Kingdom should not be taken as alarmist. To the cost of having somebody out of work may be added the cost of social multipliers: the drug taking, neurosis, inter-personal violence, decline of inner city areas and illnesses which are directly related to unemployment. Thus we will see increasingly contradictions between the micro-efficiency of the multinationals as they render work processes more capital intensive rather than labour intensive, and the awful inefficiency at the macro-level of the nation-state which then has to pick up the bill for those so displaced.

Lucas 'Everywhere'

These councils which build upon and extend the ideas developed by the Lucas workers (themselves an extension of trade union activities in Italy, the Green Bands movement in Australia and elsewhere), are beginning to demonstrate if as yet only in a modest fashion that there are alternatives to these problems. The alternatives will not be handled successfully in a 'top-down' way but only if they involve masses of people in great democratic movements where their skill and ability is released to create a future which for them is meaningful and fulfilling.

Above all else, such work is helping people to understand that the future is not out there in the sense in which a coastline might be out there before you go to discover it. Rather, the future doesn't have pre-determined shapes and forms and contours but has to be built by ordinary people, thus involving real choices. So we might breathe back into socialism some of the life, excitement and creativity which should always have been central to its very essence. A form of socialism which means more freedom rather than less, more involvement of people rather than less. It could move us away from that awful moribund form of socialism which has become repugnant to so many people. Perhaps it is only 'socialists' who could have made socialism so incredibly boring. It could be quite different — and the experiments in London, Sheffield and elsewhere are a move in that direction.

References

Cooley, M.J.E., *Architect or Bee*. Langley Tech. Services, Slough, Berks. 1981.
Wainwright, H. and Elliott, D., *The Lucas Plan*. Allison & Busby, London. 1982.
Cooley, M.J.E., *Problem of New Technology: Some Human Centred Solutions*.
  T.P.G. Faculty of Technology, Open Univ. Milton Keynes. 1982.

CHAPTER TWO

Sheffield City Council Employment Department

What follows is a set of extracts from documents produced by the Department about their aims and priorities for a programme of action.

Launching the Programme: the Political Context

The return of a Conservative government is likely to herald the continuation of the plans to privatise British Telecom, the British Transport Dock Board, the oil interest of British Gas, the profitable subsidiaries of British Rail and the wholesale dismemberment of the British Steel Corporation.

There will also be a further influx of private contracting firms into central and local government services, partly as a consequence of centrally imposed reductions in the budgets of democratically elected local authorities. Previous evidence of privatisation from Southend, Wandsworth and other local authorities suggests that these new initiatives will mean redundancies, deterioration in terms and conditions of those workers left, and decreased quantity and quality of service.

The further privatisation of welfare provision will make life on the dole more intolerable and will in itself reinforce the deflationary impact of government policy. There will develop a growing wageless sector, whose nature and numbers are concealed under various headings: the "hidden unemployed" will include "enforced housewives", unregistered unemployed, the prematurely retired, and those forced to give up work (or unable to obtain work) because they must look after dependants at home. Coupled with others who are not in the formal economy — notably the retired — this will mean a very large and growing number of people in the weakest position within society. These trends will be made worse by the undermining of measures which have increased access to the labour market, including employment protection legislation and nursery provision. There will also be moves to develop a "family policy" which attempts to shift part of the welfare state into the home, to redomesticate women and to tackle youth unemployment in part by increasing parental accountability for "unrest".

These government policies over the past four years have not succeeded in reversing the decline of UK industry. British industrial production has stagnated, even compared with other industrialised countries. The level of UK manufacturing production in 1982 was the lowest since 1967 while for the first time in peace-time, since the industrial revolution, Britain imported more manufactured goods than it exported. Manufacturing investment, the key to future projects, remains extremely low, inhibited by low demand and high interest rates. Manufacturing investment fell by 10 per cent in 1981 and by mid 1982 had fallen by a further four per cent.

Sheffield has had a tradition of unemployment levels below the national average until the late 1970s. This reflected the relative strength of an industrial base centred on heavy manufacturing (steel and engineering) reinforced in the 1960s and 1970s by the growth of service industries like banking and distribution.

In the last three years, the situation has changed dramatically with an unprecedented collapse of industry. There are now fewer jobs in the city than in 1979; between January 1980 and January 1983 41,000 redundancies were announced, of which 82 per cent were in manufacturing. And the number of unfilled job vacancies has declined; in June 1983 there was just one vacancy for every 55 people claiming Unemployment Benefit. The rate of unemployment *tripled* in the three years between 1979 and 1982 and in June 1983 stood at 13.7 per cent, 1.4 per cent above the national average.

From the early 1970s it has been restructuring and rationalisation of steel, engineering and the related industries which produced the major job losses. More recently, the decline in local manufacturing has ceased to be cushioned by a growth in service jobs as the service sector has also started to shed jobs over the past two years. So employment and unemployment trends need to be set in the context of industrial changes; these are not merely local and temporary. They are a reflection of long term structural changes in the industries dominating the local economy and of a national and international recession, particularly marked since 1979. These have been exacerbated by central government policy, and are, in part, facilitated by fundamental technological changes.

Why a Sheffield Employment Department?

The response from the labour movement to the increasing de-industrialisation has, hitherto, appeared muted. In some cases this reflects the fear that opposition may lead to redundancies or closure and it will be impossible to get another job. By and large, also, the labour movement does not have the access to the resources of finance or skills that help provide alternatives. This problem is often made worse by the fact that the response which is possible to technological change implemented by the owners of industry rather than those who work in industry is often too late to offset its consequences.

Setting the economic crisis of Sheffield within its national and international context can, too easily, lead to the conclusion that there is indeed no alternative. What it identifies, however, is the necessity to provide concrete practical examples of alternatives to the government policies which have reinforced the drastic decline of industry and jobs.

Sheffield is the first local authority in the UK (perhaps in Europe) to create an Employment Committee and an Employment Department. Its aims are ambitious; to co-ordinate everything that the City Council can do to help:

i. to prevent further loss of jobs in the City;
ii. to alleviate the worst effects of unemployment, and to encourage effective training for new skills and jobs;
iii. to stimulate new investment, to create new kinds of employment, and to diversify job opportunities in the City;
iv. to explore new forms of industrial democracy and co-operative control over work.

The immediate reason for setting up an Employment Committee is, of course, the rapid rise in unemployment and the crisis facing Sheffield's traditional industries. However, the longer-term aim is to try to gain more direct, local, democratic control over employment, and to impose a greater degree of social planning upon the structural and technological changes taking place in Sheffield, along with many other manufacturing communities.

Several other authorities (notably the GLC and the West Midlands County Council) have begun to take similar initiatives, but these are mainly at the regional rather than the local level (and therefore concerned with economic and industrial development in rather more general terms). By focusing in on "employment" Sheffield is pioneering new territory for local government and as yet there are very few examples to follow. We should not under-estimate the potential importance of this development. It is likely that by the end of the 80's it will be as familiar for a local authority to have an Employment Committee and Department, as it currently is to have education, housing, family and community services etc.

The thrust of the Employment Department's effort must go, therefore, into fieldwork rather than into headquarters management. The Department's most skilled staff will be in the field, leading the exploration and innovation *themselves*, rather than supervising less experienced junior staff from the headquarters. This kind of less hierarchical, more collective inter-disciplinary project-work is familiar in many research and development situations in industry, and in action-research projects.

Strategies

The central requirement for Sheffield's Employment initiatives is for a 'counter-offensive' against the forces and ideas which construct the current employment situation and the climate in which it is discussed.

This counter-offensive must be built around practical examples which challenge the argument that "there is no alternative". Our alternatives cannot, however, be built in isolation, nor planned in haste; any more than 'workers' plans' spring up overnight as a reaction to the threat of redundancies. Such alternatives arise out of campaigns for better working conditions or services and in dialogue between workers in different departments or firms, those who want to work, and those who use these services or products.

Nor will these practical examples, in themselves, reverse the national and international trends already documented. They will, however, provide models of alternative ways of organising production and use to ensure that unmet social needs are catered for outside the mechanism of the market. In the process they will provide workers and users with the experience both of what alternatives are possible, and of the organisation that is necessary to put them into practice.

Even for this modest appraisal of the possibilities of economic alternatives the resources of the Employment Department are inadequate. There is an immediate need to identify a limited number of strategies within which specific projects or proposals can be directed and developed in order to maximise the use of resources available.

Public Sector Priorities

PRIORITY ONE — *Campaigns Against Local Authority Expenditure Cuts and Privatisation*

The threat to local authority employment and services has been outlined. A central objective of the Employment Programme Committee in 1983/84 will be to develop the campaigns against further cuts and privatisation with unions, the workforce, and users of the services inside the authority, through a substantial education and research programme.

PRIORITY TWO — *The Quality of Services and Conditions of Employment in the Authority*

Detailed discussion of the quality of existing services and the experience of workers in their employment by the Authority will need to be closely integrated with the campaigns against further privatisation. Already, four projects have been developed in this area:
  i. the Positive Action programme, set up in conjunction with the Personnel Department, illustrates the importance of equal opportunities particularly for women, and ethnic minorities;
  ii. the low pay campaign, concentrating on the quality and distribution of employment opportunities in the Local Authority;
  iii. the Town Hall model of the Youth Training Scheme, defending and expanding local authority employment within the context of high quality training;
  iv. the development and use of new technology to improve both.

PRIORITY THREE — *The Council's Role in the Local Economy*

As well as being the largest single employer in the city, the Council is a major investor and purchaser of goods and services. The Council's Housing Department Capital Programme for 1983/84 is £48.5m and in meeting social needs for housing, shelter and warmth, provides employment for building workers in the Works Department and private firms. This particular area of work will be developed in the coming year by:
  i. analysis of employment consequences of the expenditure of all Local Authority Departments both inside the Authority and in the city as a whole;
  ii. more specifically, the impact of the Housing Department's capital programme;
  iii. an analysis of the employment consequences and social need provision of the Family & Community Services Department.

PRIORITY FOUR — *Identification of Unmet Social Need and Development of Projects to Meet this Need and Provide Employment*

Together with those groups whose needs are not currently being met in the city (tenants, pensioners, women, ethnic minorities, the unemployed and others) and those workers or potential workers whose knowledge and skills should enable them to be met, the following projects could be developed:
  i. work on housing needs and the needs of the disabled and elderly;
  ii. the development of products to meet social needs in the Third World, and providing local employment;
  iii. work on the Sheffield Employment Plan showing that it is possible to generate economic activity to meet unmet social need without job substitution. This means campaigning around a new emphasis to the use of Community Programme schemes and developing the arguments around the social uselessness of unemployment;
  iv. work on the Scotia Project as meeting the needs of unemployed youngsters with musical talents;
  v. work on the possible development of a Combined Heat and Power Station for Sheffield. This is currently at the feasibility study stage;
  vi. central to all these initiatives on the development of projects and alternative models to provide for unmet social needs is the work of the Product Development Company and SCEPTRE.

Private and Nationalised Industries Sector Priorities

PRIORITY FIVE — *The provision of aid and assistance to small businesses in the private sector*

The modified Aids to Enterprises schemes will need to be reassessed in the light of the overall impact of Council involvement on local small businesses. There is, in particular, a need to look more systematically at the cutlery industry and the potential role of the local authority.

The success in attracting the National Union of Mineworkers Headquarters to Sheffield indicates that part of a redirected programme might be more directly aimed at attracting organisations whose objectives are consistent with those of the City Council.

Development of training initiatives in the private sector lies within the context of an overall training strategy which meets the objectives of the Employment Programme Committee.

These projects will be developed in conjunction with all those organisations who share the objectives of the City Council. These will include trade unions, employees' organisations, and Sheffield Trades Council.

A major feature will be the integration of equal opportunities policies into all aspects of training.

PRIORITY SIX — *Provision of Aid and Assistance to Workers' Co-operatives and Equal Opportunities Initiatives*

Initial work on a number of schemes has been developed within the Aids to Enterprises programme; schemes are now also being worked up within other Departmental programmes.

Training schemes such as the Women's Training workshop, the Engineering Co-operatives and the Asian Welfare Association, demonstrate on a small scale how the needs of disadvantaged groups can be addressed within a more planned local economic and political strategy.

PRIORITY SEVEN — *Public Sector Schemes involving the use of Private Sector Finance*

The City Council has the responsibility for setting out the overall planning framework for area development. In Sheffield there are two major initiatives being undertaken at present: the Lower Don Valley project and the Central Area District Plan. Private sector funds will be needed to augment City Council resources within a co-ordinated strategy.

The Employment Department will have a significant role in developing both initiatives to implement the Employment Programme Committee's policies in conjunction with the other Departments in the Authority.

Training schemes offer other possibilities for attracting private sector finance behind public sector initiatives and involvement.

Equal Opportunities in Employment

Up until now this document has discussed unemployment as if it were uniformly distributed throughout the population. However, statistics show that working-class people are heavily over-represented, and that unskilled and semi-skilled working-class people are hit hardest of all. Furthermore, unemployment is neither colour-blind, or sex-blind.

Unemployment among women is rising much faster than among men. Since 1975 male unemployment has risen by 61 per cent but female unemployment has risen by 207 per cent.

Women are more vulnerable to unemployment for all kinds of reasons. They often work in low-paid, insecure, part-time jobs, or temporary jobs with high labour turnover. (17 per cent of working women are clerks or cashiers; 9 per cent shop assistants; 9 per cent secretaries; 5 per cent maids; 5 per cent cleaners and 4½ per cent nurses.) Discrimination is still common and in a time of high unemployment women are often the first to lose their jobs.

Unemployment among ethnic minorities is also much higher than average. Male unemployment in England in 1977-78 among whites born in the UK was 5.3 per cent but for non-whites it was 12.3 per cent. The situation may be even worse than this as so many non-whites (like women) do not register as unemployed.

Unemployment among the disabled and handicapped is also considerably above average, and in spite of official quotas it is increasingly hard for them to find employment.

Of the above categories, women are by far the largest in number, both in the workforce (40 per cent) and among the unemployed (30 per cent). The Employment Department will co-ordinate closely with other Departments on the employment needs and opportunities for ethnic groups and the disabled, but will concentrate its own work initially mainly on the employment needs and opportunities for women.

Thinking and work about unemployment within the City Council (in common with other agencies) has tended up until now to concentrate on the traditional manufacturing industries, and to be pre-occupied with the needs of male workers. The Employment Department is appointing an Equal Opportunities Officer to try to compensate for this bias both in our ideas and analysis, and in our job-creation proposals. The main thrust of this job will be to analyse the employment needs of women and to stimulate jobs which meet those needs better.

It should be remembered that at a time of high unemployment, an "equal opportunities" policy can only be successful if it involves positive action in favour of women, and that means that in the short-term at least, men may lose out! However, the struggle for equal opportunities by women has been posing fundamental questions about the inter-connections between work, home life, personal relationships and leisure, from which both men and women will gain in the long term.

Objectives here should be:

i. To identify the nature and scale of unemployment among women. This is not easy as the official unemployment statistics do not in any way represent the real position (e.g. because of their reluctance to register officially, or their involvement in unwaged domestic labour). A good deal of survey and interview work therefore may be necessary to

define the need for employment among women.
ii. To take steps to ensure that a women's perspective is maintained on the various employment-creating proposals that are developed within the City Council, or brought forward for financial assistance;
iii. To develop specific employment projects that better meet the needs of women. This may involve retraining, or training in specific skills which previously may have been exclusive to men. There may be value in small-scale pilot and demonstration projects to "pre-figure" larger-scale possibilities for development. Funding for these may need to be sought from central and European government agencies.
iv. In conjunction with the Personnel and other service departments, to explore the role of the local authority as a major employer with a high proportion of women, mostly in the less senior positions; and to develop practical proposals to make it easier for women to take up the equal opportunities offered. In this respect, the challenge is for the local authority to become a "model employer" setting a lead for the private sector;
v. To develop similar work on the employment needs of ethnic groups and the disabled when staff resources are made available.

Review of the First Year's Work (1983)

Some would argue that for a local authority to set up a new Employment Committee and Department, in the middle of the severest economic crisis for 50 years is like David trying to tackle Goliath. (Even more cynically, others have argued that this is as useless as re-arranging deck-chairs on the *Titanic*.) Several basic points can be made however:

a. It is, after a year's work, clearly unrealistic to imagine that a small local authority department, with a budget of only £2½m, and a staff of less than 50, can by itself make a sufficient impact upon the local economy to compensate for the landslide loss of jobs through plant closures, redundancies, new technology and cuts in public expenditure and services. Over the past year, jobs in Sheffield have been lost at the rate of about 1,000 a month. This can be expected to increase over the next year if the Government's plans for privatisation of British Steel and other public corporations and services go ahead, together with further severe cuts in the resources and powers of local authorities. It is obviously essential for the City Council to continue to do everything it possibly can to defend and promote jobs in both the public and private sectors; but it is not realistic to expect to be able to keep pace with the rate of loss of jobs, or to measure the effectiveness of the City Council's contribution purely in terms of the *numbers* of jobs preserved or created.

b. Nevertheless, the exploratory work carried out by the various project teams in the first year indicates that there is no shortage of opportunities for useful and fruitful intervention by the local authority. A wide range of potential programmes and projects have been identified in each of the fields explored by the project teams. While not capable of matching the scale of job-loss facing the city, many of these can demonstrate or provide constructive alternative ways for tackling the problems we face.

c. The central question for the Employment Committee and Department, therefore, (if we are to avoid spreading our limited resources thinly and ineffectively over too wide a field) is how to concentrate the local authority's efforts behind a smaller number of key programmes and projects, co-ordinated together for maximum impact as part of a focused strategy.

CHAPTER THREE

Popular Planning and the Greater London Council

Hilary Wainwright

The Greater London Council 'Jobs for a Change' Festival 9 June 1984: over 80,000 punks, skins, unemployed blacks and other angry Londoners crowded into the august marble buildings of County Hall to dance to reggae music, to see exhibitions of co-ops, stalls of campaigns and research projects, and to debate and talk about, amongst other things, the abolition of the GLC, the miners' strike. The grand staircase to the Council Chamber, in the past strictly reserved for councillors and VIPs, was swarming with unemployed kids. The praesidium in the Council Chamber (in the past the seat only of the Director General and the Chairman of the Council) became the platform for women from the mining communities of South Yorkshire to address hundreds of Londoners.

The Festival was an event symbolic of the present GLC's use of the state resources over which they have some control. It was a vivid physical expression of the attempt to open up a part of the state and its resources to the majority of people who have no wealth or individual power. Town and County Halls have always been open to the local Chamber of Commerce, the Rotary Club and visiting businessmen and politicians. But the majority of people go to municipal buildings only as supplicants, to plead a case or to protest against hostile treatment. They go as if on to alien territory, not even sure that they will be allowed in. Certainly this has been the normal experience of London's County Hall.

How is the GLC 'Different'?

It is more than the use of the buildings that has changed. It is also a matter of who benefits and who controls the resources and powers administered within those buildings. Most people assume they have no right to public money. It has taken a lot of encouragement to get womens groups and organisations of the unemployed, for instance, to apply for funds. The same applies to GLC powers to regulate land use. Few community groups and trade unions would think that land use planning powers could be used in their favour without massive pressure and protest. Businesses, by contrast, take loans and rent-free factories for granted. As far as planning permission is concerned, a word in the right ear will normally be enough to safeguard their interests.

Labour and Tory local authorities have not been very different in these respects. Even when the content of Labour policies are more benevolent towards local people it is a philanthropic benevolence carried out on their *behalf* rather than in any direct way under their *control*. And as a result the benevolence can disappear overnight.

The Labour GLC has begun to build up a different kind of relationship with working, or would-be working, Londoners. It has not gone far enough, particularly with its own workforce, and it has been developed *ad hoc*, without any very clear sense of direction. But it has established precedents which will be important for other local authorities and even national governments with socialist aspirations. There are also many lessons that can be learnt so that future moves in this direction can be more confident and determined.

The approach varies from Council committee to committee. Common to most — ethnic minority, police, women, planning, industry and employment, and arts and recreation — is a commitment to provide grants to independent organisations as part of the making and implementing of GLC policy in that area. Thus local police monitoring committees are funded by the GLC Police Committee not as an act of benevolence but as part of the GLC's strategy for achieving democratic accountability of the Metropolitan Police. Similarly trade union research and resource centres are funded as part of GLC efforts to help trade unionists develop strategies and bargaining positions for their industries and services.

Decision making structures have changed too. The Women's Committee includes representatives nominated by feminist groups throughout London. They report back to mass meetings of women.

Joint work on policy and on campaigns between the GLC and working class organisations is another feature of the new approach. The Industry and Employment Committee, for instance, intends to work closely with trade unions and community organisations to develop, implement and where necessary fight for plans and demands that counter the destructive forces of the market. The extent, though, to which these intentions are carried out is still uneven.

This approach is not necessarily the same as the growing tendency among Labour local authorities to decentralise services. Decentralisation is concerned primarily with improving the accessibility and responsiveness of state services. It does not usually involve any significant shift in power. Power remains at the centre. The approach being developed by the GLC — and as far as I know in Sheffield — is intended to change power relations. It involves both sharing power with community and workplace organisations and helping to build their power. The end result, at least in theory, is an alliance around policies worked out together — an alliance with more power than either the GLC would have on its own, or the extra parliamentary organisations would have without political backing and resources.

In some ways such alliances have been a matter of necessity for the GLC to persist with its manifesto policies. To have any hope of maintaining policies of cheap fares, job creation and the defence of services in the face of Thatcherism, the present leadership of the GLC had to transform the role of County Hall and its relationship with the majority of Londoners. This imperative has become even more apparent in the face of the threat to the GLC itself. Like Clay Cross in the 70s and Poplar in the 30s, its commitment to its manifesto required it to become part of the opposition to central government rather than behaving as a lower tier of the state, almost an arm of government managing services and regulating land uses. The only alternative would have been to trim and to compromise in the face of government pressures in the way that many other would-be radical Labour local authorities, and under international pressures, all Labour governments have done.

Trimming and compromise are always lurking in the background. Sometimes they influence events. There are strong pressures in this direction amongst senior officers who have known little else under previous administrations. Moreover, the Labour majority is slim, and within it the position of the Left can be precarious. Then of course there are defeats because the alliances of resistance have not been sufficiently strong. The elimination of GLC control over London Transport is the most notable defeat. The ultimate defeat, abolition, remains around the corner.

The Background: Socialism and Popular Organisation

Whatever the outcome of the struggle over abolition, the GLC experience could have a historic importance for achieving socialism in Britain. The pressure of necessity to use a part of the state as a tool of resistance, combined with the leadership's political support for movements and campaigns based outside municipal politics, is helping to shape a very different image of socialism from that which has dominated Labour politics in postwar years.

The conventional popular image of socialism is associated with a strong bureaucratic state centralising power and more often than not failing to produce lasting benefits for the majority of people. This image comes partly from the experience of the Soviet Union. It also comes from the experience of Labour governments. These governments, from 1945 onwards have neither been strong against the market and the power of private capital nor supportive, open and in alliance with working class people and their organisations. Their relationship with trade unions has in practice been about controlling wages demands rather than sharing power or building new forms of working class power. It is not surprising then that Labour and Socialism has seemed in its own way part of the establishment, not to be trusted, part of 'them' rather than working with 'us'. Even the policies of the 1945 Government, which made considerable improvements in working class living standards, involved little or no shift in power or control. When the pressures of recession and the International Monetary Fund threatened even these improvements, Labour in government had created no basis for joint resistance and it had no will to resist. It took on the responsibility for the cuts, the deflation and the support for the City. In doing so it associated Labour and socialism in the popular mind with constraints, restrictions, false promises and defence of the wealthy.

Genuine socialists in the Labour Party have been unable to break this association. Partly because they themselves were part of it. Partly because they are not able to demonstrate an alternative. Tony Benn has come nearest to symbolising an alternative with his explicit and practical support for resistance: for workers occupying against closures and putting forward their own alternatives, for women taking direct action against Cruise missiles, for miners taking strike action to save their communities. But as a minority and often a marginal voice in the parliamentary party he has only been able to sow the seeds of a different vision.

Ken Livingstone and the GLC leadership from their position of real power, albeit extremely limited, have been able to take this further. They have managed to achieve at least in London an image of socialism associated with freedom and choice for people who have never had it, diversity and individuality, popular self confidence and even a degree of popular power.

The necessity of basing socialism on popular organisations rather than relying on a central state apparatus is particularly clear as far as the economy is concerned. A socialist economic strategy must aim to transform production. Changes in distribution or in circulation do not transform the direction or motor of the economy. For that motor is made up of the mechanisms of production, its drive consists of the way that the means of production are deployed, for what purposes and in whose interests. Only democratic control over how people's labour time is spent and how physical productive resources are allocated will change the motor of the economy from the accumulation of private profit to production for social needs.

But production involves a vast number of specialised, skilled processes, and the direction of production is in part a matter of how these processes are organised. Changing the direction or motor of production therefore cannot be simply a matter of changing the ownership of the means of production and placing them in the hands of political masters or mistresses with a commitment to the new direction. The new direction requires the active co-operation and initiative of those involved in the detail of the production process.

Changing Local Authorities: Some Problems

The workers' 'tacit knowledge' as Mike Cooley calls it, or 'the gold in the mind of the worker' as Japanese industrialists call the same thing (for rather different reasons) is an essential condition for planning an economy both democratically and efficiently. And it cannot be simulated by government departments. Without the direct involvement of the popular organisations that can express and co-ordinate these skills and this knowledge, all the planning agreements, state directives and industrial inspectorates in the world cannot stave off industrial collapse or prevent top management from continuing to behave according to the ways of the private market or according to their own self interest. The experience of Chile, the failure of the last Labour Government's planning agreements and the waste and corruption in the Soviet Union are all in different ways illustrations of the limits and the disasters of state intervention without an active popular base.

The GLC as a regional authority lacking even those limited powers over the economy of central government viz the power over the supply and value of money, power to take companies into public ownership against the owners wishes, power to control international trade, is even more dependent on popular initiatives and the bargaining power and political pressure that they can exert.

However, the history of many local authorities, the training and roles of their officers, the experience of many of their citizens of neglect and insensitivity weigh heavily against the possibility of steering the local authority machine to work in alliance with popular movements and organisations.

First there are problems in how the alliance is established when on the one hand local authority officers see themselves as at best responding and more often containing and diffusing popular pressure, and when local people are full of suspicion and cynicism fully justified by previous experience. The GLC experiment leads us to ask what changes have to be made within the machinery of local government in order to put into practice the political — sometimes rhetorical — commitment to transform local authorities from being the local tier of state management to being part of local resistance to state and private management. These changes I shall argue require more than the will of a group of determined politicians, though without such a group change would be impossible. What wider conditions are necessary for these changes to be achieved?

Then there are the dangers that arise when the local authority with its new commitments to strengthen popular resistance moves in, with its big boots and grand intentions, to support local initiatives which however determined in their aims are often weak in their organisation. An important part of the potential strength of initiatives and organisations at the base, whether in the workplace or the community is their independence from management or the state and their dependence on and accountability to the people whose needs they express. How can local authority funds, expertise, information and political clout be used to support such organisations without at the same time undermining their independence and democratic base?

A related question which must be asked, especially from the point of view of popular and working class organisations themselves, is in what ways can the local authority be a source of support? What is it exactly that local authority support can add to the power of trade union and community action? The answers to this question help us to work out what demands to make of a sympathetic local authority, and what limits to set on their involvement.

The Docklands Case: i) Beginning

A discussion of the case of the fight for the future of the Royal Docks, a part of London's Docklands and the role of the GLC in this struggle provides an illustration of at least some of the answers to these questions.

In October 1981 the Port of London Authority finally put an end to cargo handling in the Royal Docks, the last of London's upstream docks. It had been running down these docks for 20 years or more. In November 1981 the London Docklands Development Corporation (LDDC) — a Government-appointed urban development corporation — announced its support for a proposal by Mowlems to build a Short Take Off and Landing airport (a STOLport) in these docks. The scheme fitted well with the LDDC's aim of turning Docklands to the service of the City and with its strategy of grandiose image building projects to attract the City investors.

After hearing accidentally of promotional meetings held for selected community 'leaders', two local women, both secretaries of local tenants associations made it their business to find out more about this STOLport; the kind of aircraft it would use, the companies behind it and the associated plans of the LDDC. They were alarmed by what they discovered and soon found others who shared their concern. Although the airport was promoted on the basis of the Dash 7, a relatively quiet aircraft, many people suspected that Mowlem's intention, having got planning permission on this basis would then allow helicopters, commuter jets and generally the sort of traffic that the airport would require to become and to remain profitable.

Even the Dash 7 would be an intrusion and a threat to the safety and peace of mind of local people, many of whom live literally the other side of the wall to the proposed airport site. But they might have been prepared to accept these costs if there had been any convincing evidence that the airport would bring jobs and prosperity for local people. At present one in every four adults in Newham's Docklands is on the dole. There was no shortage of claims and promises of jobs from Mowlems and the LDDC; claims which were regularly headlined in the local paper, and won the airport considerable local support. But there was very little hard evidence. Certainly, the majority of trade unions were not convinced and they joined with Connie Hunt and Lil Hopes, the two women who started the questioning, and planners from the Joint Dockland Action Group, the local trade union and community resource centre, to launch the Campaign Against the Airport.

Around this time, autumn 1981, the GLC's Industry and

Employment Committee created its Popular Planning Unit, whose brief was to provide resources and political support to unions and community groups developing their own plans or positive bargaining positions as part of the struggle to defend or create jobs. The unit was staffed not by people trained in local government, but by people with experience of research and campaigning in unions or communities.

At that early stage organisations were not exactly knocking on the door of the Popular Planning Unit for support. Few organisations, besides those in close touch with leading GLC politicians, had any expectation that the GLC would share resources with outside groups or give political backing to plans and campaigns developed outside County Hall. Though 'grants' were mentioned in Labour's manifesto they were not a priority and there was no clear strategy behind the idea. Moreover, the Livingstone administration was not swept into power by a groundswell of popular pressure. It had popular support, mainly for its transport policy of 'Fares Fair', but its victory was not a political reflection of the sort of strong and self confident shop floor trade unionism that led to the alternative plan at Lucas Aerospace. Trade unionism in many of London's workplaces, especially in manufacturing and traditional industries like the docks, was defeated and demoralised. Yet popular planning depends on resistance and struggle. Indeed resistance is its starting point; its base is popular action and organisation not any part of the State. Unlike the traditional local authority consultation processes, local authority support for popular planning involves unlocking and using the resources of the local state to back up and spread community or workplace based initiatives, rather than to organise a state controlled and defined framework of debate.

The priority then for the Popular Planning Unit was to identify where within the priority areas laid out in Labour's manifesto was community or trade union action taking place with implications for jobs. What kind of support could the GLC give to this action? Was the action at a point where the groups concerned were moving on to the offensive and thinking about their own alternatives?

Docklands was a high priority in the Industry and Employment section of the manifesto. And with the LDDC in control over all planning development, the possibility of the GLC having a significant effect on employment prospects in Docklands was even more dependent on an alliance with community and trade union organisations. However, when we talked of 'popular planning' to activists in Docklands, a glazed look came over their eyes. There had been so many well intentioned 'strategic plans', 'planning processes' and 'planning consultation', all with their own gimmicks and sweeteners. Why should the GLC's proclamations of support for popular planning be any different? It was only when we became involved in the Campaign Against the Airport, attending the public meetings in the Three Crowns, North Woolwich, joining in the steering group discussions in Lil Hopes' front room, that 'popular planning' began to make any distinct practical sense.

Our first job, before any talk of alternatives, was simply to make sure that the GLC promptly took a strong public position against the airport. Achieving that was the necessary basis of working together on anything more. The GLC's early opposition to the airport was important to the campaign. It helped counterbalance the influence of the LDDC on Newham Council, which at one point looked to be favouring the airport. The final vote was 37 to 18 against the airport. GLC opposition and direct contact with the campaign meant that the considerable technical resources of the GLC, its noise experts in particular and also its economists and planners could be harnessed to the case against the airport and later on to the development of the alternative, the People's Plan. It added to the pressure on the Minister of State for the Environment to call a Public Inquiry. It opened up the possibility of getting funds to enable the Campaign to have the best possible legal representation at this inquiry. It laid the basis for developing the GLC's economic strategy for the area in a way that was based on the ideas of the people who live and work in Docklands.

The Docklands Case: ii) Creating the Alternative

The decision to develop an alternative came out of the Campaign's experience. Time and time again as it tried to extend local support it came up against the argument: 'Well, they say it will bring jobs, and there is no alternative is there?' A campaign meeting was set aside to discuss "Our alternative for employment". The Popular Planning Unit offered to provide whatever funds were necessary to develop convincing alternative plans. The concern of both the Campaign and the Popular Planning Unit was to draw up the alternative in a way that would help to extend support for the campaign and build the ability of the Newham Docklands Forum, a local federation of trade union and community groups, to fight for the alternative plans.

The Forum took responsibility for the alternative plan so that the campaign could concentrate on building up the case against the airport. There was some overlap of members. Each organisation was affiliated to the other. But there was a practical division of labour between leading individuals. This was important because the ambitious idea of an alternative plan could otherwise have swamped the more basic tasks of the campaign.

The Forum decided what they needed from the GLC: funds for a shopfront centre in a central shopping parade; funds to employ a team of local people to go round the area encouraging people to contribute ideas and comments; funds for publicity material to let people know that the plan was in preparation and their views were welcome.

The Popular Planning Unit released these funds — £14,000 in total for six months — by using local government powers for carrying out research and disseminating information. As with much of the Industry and Employment Committee's work there is no legal framework for the GLC's support for popular planning; it requires improvising with existing laws. The funds were agreed in March 1982. The public inquiry was to start in May and the campaign's lawyers calculated that the People's Plan could be presented at any time from July, though September seemed most likely.

The Forum had less than six months in which to prepare their alternative plan. They had never done anything like this before. The People's Plan Centre — five workers, three part-time, two full-time — were local people with detailed knowledge of the area and the needs of particular groups but with no experience of a project quite like this. One, Tracy Hastings, was only leaving school in May, but she had strong views on the need for water sports facilities to use the docks and the river. Two, Daphne Clarke and Annette Fry, were local mothers both involved in local childcare groups and other projects such as a Toy Library, concerned with children. Bill Hart, a 53 year old ex-tugman had a deep commitment to seeing the docks used in some way for shipping and boat building. Gary Cooke, a young ex-T&GWU shop steward, was interested in projects that would exploit new technology in a socially useful way.

They tried a variety of ways of reaching people, learning from their mistakes, and from poor responses, to find more direct means of contact. First letters went out to all official organisations, tenants associations, trade union branches and so on. Only a few responded. So then they went round more informal groups: mothers and toddlers, keep fit classes, even speaking in the interval at bingo sessions in a local community

centre. They visited all the 75 companies still in docks. They
talked to workers in the local bus garage and visited shop
stewards in the few remaining factories in Silvertown, outside
the dock wall. Sometimes they simply knocked on doors and
carried out doorstep interviews. One idea which worked well
was 'Surgeries' on each estate. They gave out leaflets to every
house and said that the People's Plan workers would be holding
a surgery between 2-6 pm at the local community centre or
tenants hall to hear people's ideas.

The Popular Planning Unit's role in this first stage of
gathering ideas and information was small. They helped the
People's Plan Centre to produce two copies of a newspaper that
reported on the development of the plan. It was delivered to
every house in the area — around 10,000 in all. The Unit became
more involved at the second stage of carrying forward and
follow-up research on the ideas that came out of this initial
process. This included researching the possibilities for boat
building and ship repair activities for which the docks were
ideally suited with two workable dry docks; and research on the
employment implications of meeting the local needs for child
care and care of the elderly that the initial discussions had
identified; and arranging research on the cost and technicalities
of converting a large warehouse into a local sports centre.

The GLC had already, prior to the announcement of the
airport, commissioned an economist's report on the prospects
for a small cargo handling operation in the Royal Docks. It came
up with conclusions very similar to those put forward by
dockers' shop stewards when they were fighting the closure of
the docks in the mid 70s. Discussions with dockers at a T&GWU
dockers educational week during the preparation of the People's
Plan improved these ideas. A closer relationship between the
dockers and the economic consultants probably would have
meant a better report in the first place. But the report was
carried out before any kind of popular planning process had got
off the ground.

By the beginning of September the plan had been drafted and
the Newham Docklands Forum were preparing the final draft
for submission to the inquiry. It was presented as part of the
evidence of the Campaign Against the Airport by 14 different
witnesses. The GLC also incorporated its main themes into their
evidence.

The Docklands Case: iii) The People's Plan

The content of the plan, as well as the method, reflected the
alliance between local groups and the GLC. Originating as it did

from the Campaign Against the Airport, its focus is land use in Newham, and its first aim is to show that there is an alternative use of the docks that makes better use of local resources in the interests of local people. But its main industrial proposal for a transport and distribution centre values the local resources from the point of view of their contribution to the wider needs of Londoners and the London economy. It stresses the unique opportunity that this interchange of water, road and rail transport could offer London, by enabling freight to go on to the river and reducing the pressure of lorry traffic. It shows how existing timber and food processing industries could be expanded by using public sector purchasing to achieve economies of scale. For example, the plan proposed the building of a joint Direct Labour joinery workshop and timber store for the local authorities of the East End in a part of the dock which would receive the timber by water. The plan also included a proposal for a co-operative zone which would make the most of the transport interchange and share common facilities.

The plan combines this ambitious industrial plan with detailed proposals for community use of the vast Royal Docks. Fundamental to their community plan was the idea of a bridge of land over the one dock which could be of no more use for shipping. This would unite the communities at present separated by the 900 acres of water. This land, together with existing land by the dock, would provide for a major housing development to provide council houses with gardens for rent by the thousands of tenants on waiting lists to get out of Newham's notorious tower blocks. Ronan Point where people died as a result of a gas explosion is just to the north of the dock.

A proposal in the community section of the plan which particularly captured people's imaginations was the proposal for shed 4, a vast warehouse without internal supporting structures. "Open the Door to Shed 4" is the slogan for shed 4 to be converted into a sports centre providing indoor five-a-side football, tennis, badminton and more. A local artist drew several pictures illustrating what such a conversion would look like.

Many people, women in particular, had never been beyond the dock wall. The idea of being asked what should go on inside the docks had been unthinkable. The threat of an airport made them realise that it mattered, and the discussions about the people's plan aroused strong feelings for opening up the docks to the community, knocking down the dock wall providing access to the water for local people.

The speed at which the plan was done, and perhaps the process too, has meant that the plan has only a few projects detailed enough to carry out straight from the plan. There are some of this character: shed 4 is one around which a strong local campaign has developed and already organised a weekend five-a-side football match. A women's resource and training centre is another, which has already received funding from the GLC. But the plan is less a list of projects and more an assertion of an alternative direction for Docklands to the City oriented plans of the LDDC. The People's Plan is drawing public attention to the potential of the people of Docklands and the resources they need not only to rebuild the local economy but to contribute to rebuilding London's economy.

Events in the Royal Docks since the Public Inquiry have been an increasingly explicit clash of these two directions, with the government, the LDDC and the Port of London Authority on one side and the Newham Docklands Forum, the major local unions, the GLC and rather uncertainly the local Council on the other. After the plan had been presented at the Inquiry it was presented at the GLC Industry and Employment Committee which moved one of its regular meetings out of County Hall to the Ascension Church Hall, Custom House to the north of the Royal Albert Dock. The GLC agreed to publish the plan and enable the Newham Docklands Forum to give it free to every household. It also agreed to start negotiations with the PLA for a part of the dock, the north side of the dock on which to start implementing at least the industrial proposals of the plan.

Since then the PLA has prevaricated — and initial slowness on the part of the GLC valuers allowed them to get away with it; the LDDC has stepped in to impose a Compulsory Purchase Order on the land; and the Inspector has recommended in favour of a restricted Dash 7 Stolport. The battle is not over though. The PLA has been challenged by local people, who occupied the PLA's board rooms at Tilbury with the active support of the dockers; then invited the PLA chairman to the People's Plan Centre and turned the event into a public interrogation of the PLA. A similar protest was staged against the LDDC when its new Chairman visited County Hall. GLC councillors turned the visit into a public meeting at which local people from all over Docklands turned up to question and to argue. At the time of writing the campaign for the People's Plan for the land, for shed 4, and for houses with gardens is concentrating all its attention on stopping the airport.

The Docklands Case: iv) The Implications

How the campaign will develop and what they will win cannot now be foreseen. But what is clear is that the forces challenging the arrogant power of the LDDC are far stronger than if the GLC had acted as a conventional local authority working on its own, maybe with other local authorities, but never dreaming of building up the power of local community and trade union organisations. Similarly the initiatives of local groups have been more ambitious, more confident and have achieved wider support, greater authority and a stronger political voice as a result of GLC support.

The docklands experience does not itself provide model answers to the questions asked earlier, but it does illustrate the possibilities of a new kind of alliance and as a result it is easier to see the direction in which these questions should be answered.

It illustrates both positively and negatively some of the changes in local government that are necessary: a GLC Unit staffed by people with experience of carrying out research and campaigns with trade union and community groups was vital. But it was not enough. There were difficulties in making full use of the GLC's powers in support of the Campaign Against the Airport and the People's Plan, e.g., its powers to buy land, its resources to present a case at a public inquiry, its responsibilities for the management of certain aspects of the river, which indicate that it's not enough to create new units staffed by people brought in for the purpose. There needs to be a reform and retraining of all the traditional departments, e.g, the valuers, the massive transport and planning department etc., which after all carry out some of the most powerful functions of the GLC. For this to be possible requires more than determined politicians, it also requires pressure on officers from trade union and community groups to carry through the commitments of politicians. This involves an extension of the idea of accountability. In a sense it involves extending the limited power of politicians to make the civil service accountable to extra parliamentary organisations. Certainly over the issues in Docklands, lawyers, valuers and noise specialists working on the GLC's case against the airport had on several occasions to submit to the pressure of the local campaign — which had the support of GLC councillors.

A strategy which stresses the role of democratic power beyond the elected members raises the issue of which community and trade union organisations did the GLC ally itself with and on what basis? In Newham's Docklands, there were several tenants' associations which were in favour of the airport. On one occasion they protested that they should get a grant from the GLC. But the GLC's support for the Campaign Against the Airport was not based on the populist notion that support for community groups is a good thing in itself; it was part of a strategy to carry out a specific policy: a different kind of industrial development. The strategy was based on the belief that a strong trade union and community campaign would contribute to the success of that policy. This illustrates what is meant by an alliance between the GLC and local organisations; it is an alliance based on common objectives and on the assumption that community and trade union organisations have a distinct source of power to bring to the achievement of these objectives.

This leads to the next question of how do the local community and trade union organisations involved in such an alliance avoid being crushed in the large and powerful handshake of the GLC? For example in Docklands, the People's Plan Centre depended almost entirely on its grant from the GLC. This gave the GLC immense power in relation to the local group, and looking back it was important consciously to limit the use of that power. Often this limit was imposed by the clarity of the Campaign's leadership about what they wanted from the GLC. Also the involvement of the Joint Docklands Action Group meant that the local groups never became dependent on GLC expertise and research as well as funds. However at other times the GLC's Popular Planning Unit became involved too closely with the internal management of the People's Plan Centre and its staff. The problem with this was that the GLC's funding position gave it overwhelming power in any conflict, and this potentially undermined the group's ability to resolve its problems independently. The lesson that can be drawn from this is that if an alliance is to be based on the organisational autonomy of community and trade union organisations, the local authority should avoid being directly involved in the day to day internal management of a group's affairs. Organisational independence is an important condition for the power of the alliance. Without it the popular base and therefore strength of the local or trade union groups would be easily sapped.

There are many practical and important lessons like this which must be drawn self consciously over the next few years from the experience of the GLC, Sheffield and elsewhere. They contribute to a new kind of socialist political practice, a practice that brings together the lessons learnt from and through feminism, the experiences of rank and file workers groups, the demands of militant black organisations, and the movement for political accountability in the Labour Party. The GLC experience has enabled that politics to have the backing of significant resources and power. Whether or not the Labour Party itself can learn these lessons on a national scale is very doubtful, certainly in its present form. Denis Healey welcoming a festival against cruise missiles at the Ministry of Defence? Peter Shore and Jon Silkin discussing grants to womens action groups? Gerald Kaufman suggesting support for shop stewards combine committees to draw up alternative plans for jobs? Neil Kinnock supporting funds for independent black organisations? The difficulty of even thinking of it makes you see why Labour's parliamentary support for Livingstone's GLC has not been all it should have been. Perhaps they realise that its most innovative activities contain the potential of an alternative not just to Thatcherism but to themselves.

CHAPTER FOUR

Making People Powerful: Coventry Workshop
Paul Field

This book is partly about some good ideas. It's about socially useful things — such as production for need, and winning control.

It isn't at all difficult to persuade people who don't have such ideas that making or organising for social usefulness is a good *idea*. The idea of justice or of plenty isn't difficult to put across to those suffering discrimination or poverty. But ways and means of getting there *are* difficult. Making the ideas real means demonstrating their reality and possibility in practice. It means making people powerful today so that they can take power tomorrow.

This essay looks at some of the ways in which a small organisation in Coventry tries to help make people powerful. The Workshop's own statement of purposes has been like this.

Coventry Workshop was set up in 1975 to carry out research and advisory work within the local trade union, labour and community movement. It works in close co-operation with groups of shop stewards, workers, the unemployed, tenants and residents in the City, and is accountable to the trade union and community organisations and individuals who subscribe to it. Its *aims* are:

— to support workers, the unemployed, tenants and residents, and their organisations, in their efforts to gain control collectively over their lives, and to understand the forces which deny them this control;
— to assist in examining issues faced by labour and community organisations in the workplace, at home and in the community; to investigate the relationships between these issues, and to help overcome existing divisions between trade union, labour and community organisations;
— to make relevant information and skills available to workers' and community organisations in ways which will be understandable and useful to their membership as a whole.

Workshop activities include: research and investigation; help with technical advice from specialist workers who come in not as 'experts' but as committed advisers; assistance with the organisation and action of groups in building their campaigns; informal education; the provision of library and information services; publication of a bi-monthly bulletin on campaigns, issues, legislation, events; and photocopying, typing and printing services.

According to mainstream Labour doctrine in Britain, making people powerful has meant struggling to abandon power to institutions which claim to represent a collective interest in some way. Historically, these institutions constitute a partial defeat for other — quite different — democratic traditions. These include at least one which urgently needs to be renewed now if the trade union and community movements are actually going to move anywhere but backwards. This tradition — this skill, if you like — lies in the ability to organise on the ground for change.

About Power

The ability of the exploited and oppressed to organise their knowledge and energies democratically is as important to mass political literacy today as was reading and writing earlier this century. The battle for words — for reading and writing — has, some say, been won. After all, we all go to school now and most of us learn our three R's. As a result, there is freedom of speech and thought. We have free trade unions, a free press and a parliamentary democracy. So we are told.

But what most people don't learn now is the political skill needed to organise their assault on the enemies of freedoms which still have to be won. They have yet to win the freedom to work, and eat, and live in decent homes. They still have to win the freedom to enjoy the wealth created by their labours and the power to protect their enjoyment. They've lost the political wherewithal to use the words they've learned to read, and to write the press they need to create. They've almost lost the unions they belong to and can no longer discipline the parties they sometimes vote for.

Nowhere in the state system of education are the skills of popular organisation — of how to control things democratically — taught or learned. Rarely are these skills acquired any more in everyday life. People have been *dis*organised, deskilled, by the very forces which appeared to make them free — by schools, by the press, by parliament and, it must be said, by many of their trade unions.

How can this have happened? Take one instance. Trade unionism in Britain enshrines some of the few remaining examples of a once vigorous political tradition in popular culture. It was a tradition of often militant self-activity and democracy, of struggle and of movement. It was the impulse to act against oppression and injustice wedded to a knowledge of how to do it.

The impulse for struggle is certainly still there, but the knowledge of how to act on it is no longer part of any popular heritage. In most trade unions, this instinct has been encrusted and dulled by settled routines. The forms and habits of trade unionism are now acquired by only the most dedicated, militant or ambitious. Today, for the most part, the trade union branch, the district committee, even the mass meeting, lack any real creativity or popularity. For that matter, there isn't much democracy left either, if by 'democracy' is meant mass involvement in making policy and strategy.

Strange as this may seem, these comments are not intended as attacks on the labour and trade union movements as such. Indirectly, this criticism says more about the success of white, male, capitalist power than it does about the failure of popular resistance. It bears witness to the extraordinary success with which those who rule — be they a class, sex or race — have reached a settlement with their official opposition, very largely on their own terms. The style, assumptions and organisation of a labour party or a trade union, for example, are riddled with ruling class habits. There is bureaucracy, hierarchy, double dealing and jostling for position. Knowledge is monopolised, new ideas are stifled and mass agitation discouraged. These are all ruling class tricks.

In recognising these faults on our own side, however, we simply acknowledge the ingenuity with which the enemy has invaded and settled in our own camp. If we *have* lost ground to them in this way, then we *must* reclaim it. The argument is simply this — the tools of popular agitation and organisation need to be recovered and renewed. They need to become familiar to us. We said earlier that the impulse for struggle has been dulled by the routines of formal, representative democracy. This is only partly true. The willingness to fight does still thrive, particularly amongst those who have the least to lose. Who are they?

Since 1975, when Coventry Workshop was launched, there have been numerous examples of how the most unlikely people — tenants scattered about in 'temporary' council slums, or women working at the bottom of one or other economic pile —

have fought courageous battles with astonishing skill against all the odds. As a rule, these campaigns are lost in the end. But this is usually because the 'big guns' are never brought to the front line — in particular, the best organised industrial unions.

In Coventry, the temporary tenants' campaign did win official recognition of their disgraceful plight from the opposition Labour group on the Council, during a short spell of Tory rule between 1977 and 1979. On the face of it, these tenants were in the worst possible position from which to launch a campaign for public recognition and decent housing. They were strewn about all over the City in houses later admitted to be unfit for human habitation. They were smeared with lies about their characters and personal lives — they were poor, unemployed and depressed. Yet, once brought together by Coventry Workshop and the Trades Council, once shown they were not alone, they laid seige to the City Council. Pickets, demonstrations, prosecutions and speeches followed. Tenants serenaded a full council meeting from the public gallery — singing very rude songs about leading councillors and decorating the chamber with pretty coloured streamers. Their eventual victory was only partial. True, once returned to power, the Labour Council did formally abolish the category of 'Part 3', temporary accommodation. But the slums and the punishment block housing policy remained more or less intact.

How could the big guns have helped? Well, if just one of the larger factories — a Massey Ferguson, say, or a Talbot — had downed tools for a day in support of the tenants, the City might just have found decent homes for them. Of course, they might not. The point, however, is that the tenants couldn't sustain their campaign alone. They needed the strength of organised labour behind them. And what organised labour needed — especially when it was strong — was an understanding of struggle and solidarity beyond the workplace, beyond 'procedure'. Above all, organised workers needed to experience their power outside work — to reconnect with their other lives as residents and as tenants in the city.

The temporary tenants' campaign is properly recorded as a moment in the history of the community movement locally. But the curious thing is that the community movement doesn't really have a history at all. It doesn't have a tradition made permanent in institutions like the TUC. It doesn't have permanence, professionals or established procedure. In this sense, nobody in community struggles ever gets to know what they're doing like experts do, so everybody gets a chance to learn how to do it. They can make it up as they go along.

This missing history can make groups like tenants' associations very strong and very weak at the same time. In this way, they resemble some of the industrial disputes led by and involving women workers (Grunwick, say, or Lee Jeans). Women's history is missing too. And this can make them strong because it can mean they are more prepared to risk the daring and courage needed to battle against the odds.

One implication of all this is that strategic alliances across the boundaries of work, home and wagelessness would reinvigorate a power grown sluggish with lack of practice. The other implication is less hopeful.

Towards Popular Democracy

There is clear evidence now that a huge new 'underclass' is being created within and around the working class. This is not, of course, an unusual feature of exploitative societies — there have always been groups at the bottom of the pile. What *is* new, however, is the scale and severity of the restructuring that's going on within and around the working class — the sheer *numbers* of women, young, very old, black and poor who are being cast into a more or less permanent state of economic dependence and political subordination. Now, those parts of the trade union movement which will undoubtedly survive recent attacks on them and will certainly rebuild themselves, could well do so in a form which excludes this underclass. We could face a recovery in the strength of trade unions which will not represent the new poor, the permanently unwaged. With the assistance of the State, capitalists have always tried to pick us up and shake us out to meet their changing requirements. The problem is that if it's left to official trade union organisations, as they are presently constituted, to pick up the pieces, all they might be interested in are the relatively easy bits — like the people left in paid employment. As for the rest, well they'll have to be ministered to by a new Poor Law Commission, call it the MSC or DHSS.

Our argument suggests that the recovery of popular democracy — at the base of trade unionism in an alliance with community struggles — would help to counteract this danger. But how can people learn to recover their power? Who will teach them? One view is that the TUC should do the job. Schools won't, the Labour Party can't, and none of them will without a struggle. In the end, of course, people will teach themselves and will learn again for themselves. But they need help.

Coventry Workshop

In Coventry, there are growing signs, however faint, of a new generation of workplace activists preparing to take up this struggle. Many are quietly urging a break with old habits of trade union rivalry and sectionalism. Aware of the devastating changes which have been forced into working and communal life, they are looking for new ways. They are, for example, looking for new alliances between blue and white collar workers, and for links between the issue of *what* they are paid for their labour and *how* their labour should be used to serve the community.

Outfits like Coventry Workshop hover about on the edge of the problem of looking for new ways. We do try to offer a learning service. But we don't 'teach' the people who ask for our support. Instead, we try to draw out and draw on the knowledge, experience and skill these people already have in order to help them grow strong. After all, that is where their strength really lies.

The people who founded Coventry Workshop in the mid-1970s designed the style and content of their work around this principle — that power starts where the people are. Some of the founders had been social workers. Others were trained professionals in local government services — planners and health inspectors. All had been through four or five years working with Coventry's Community Development Project (CDP). The CDP was an experimental government programme which tried different ways of delivering community services to intractable 'problem areas' in the inner city. People who had never before worked together — social workers, planners and so on — set about solving the inner city problem (again).

The experience taught some of them to reject the professional relationship between 'expert' and 'client' and to reject the assumption that the main problem was the client herself. Instead, it became clear that this style of work served to deepen people's sense of powerlessness and damage their self confidence. Far from giving people strength, the expert service weakened any potential there might be for grassroots agitation around problems shared by whole communities. Far from the residents of places like Hillfields *being* the problem, their common position in the structure of the local economy had created problems *for* them. And no amount of individual counselling — however well packaged — could solve that. At the same time, it was obvious that some of what the 'experts' knew needed to be learned and taken over by people in the street.

The Workshop was started, then, to put these and other ideas to the test. Popular organisation needed more local resources — of research and day to day support — than were available from within existing national bodies. How could such resources be created, and how could such an initiative remain independent from any particular set of interests — be they government, trade union or political party? Clearly, if the Workshop was going to win people's trust and confidence, it had to be seen to have no other axes to grind than those carried by the people who used the service. Yet Workshop staff would have to be quite open about where they stood, whose side they were on. If it was to be a service to the local trade union and community movements, then the Workshop had to come under their control at some point. Independence from official authorities and accountability to users were essential conditions. But these could not be decreed in a charter. They had to be won by building support for the quality and integrity of the work done.

In the light of these fairly stringent conditions, Coventry Workshop was set up to test the kind of support needed by local trade union members, unemployed, tenants and residents in their efforts to gain more control over their lives at work and in the community. It would do this by:

— working with groups to provide information, research back-up and help with developing their organisations and campaigns.
— drawing out the links between workplace and community issues — showing how apparently distinct, unrelated problems may have common roots.
— fitting what was learned into an expanding picture of what was going on in the city as a whole and using that understanding to broaden people's perspective on particular issues.
— working as 'committed advisers' rather than outside experts; being careful not to create dependence and not to substitute for independent, democratic trade union or community organisations; helping people gain confidence in their ability to take more power.

Eight years on, we are still striving for independence and accountability. We piece together the money to pay six people from churches and charities, from subscriptions and donations and, more recently, from the Labour-controlled West Midlands County Council. A small number of volunteers supports almost every bit of work in one way or another. Our long term aim would be to see the kind of work and resources we offer made a permanent feature of British political and trade union activity. But the relationship between politics and trade unionism would have to be quite different for this to be possible.

In the meantime, our job is still to work with people on the issues they identify and with resources they already bring to the problem — most especially their own knowledge and skills. Where gaps in their knowledge do become clear, we can help with additional research and access to technical know-how in things like the law or publications. We can also draw on a growing network of contacts who have the experience or ideas people might need. Above all, we try to fill the gaps in people's knowledge or contacts in such a way as to make it possible for them to find out or do the unfamiliar things for themselves next time.

Our other task is always to be counted on and trusted to do the things we say we *can* do. This means we have to lay our stall out as clearly as possible when people come to us for help or when we offer it. We call this 'the contract'. In effect, we're saying to people: 'we support what you're trying to do and have some ideas about it ourselves. These are the things we can do best and these are the things we think you should be doing yourselves. Now let's put these talents together to get you where you want to be'.

The fact that we are still here eight years on has changed what we are able to do and say in the city. A growing number of trade union organisations and community groups now see the Workshop as a resource which belongs to them in some way. This means we are trusted to do a useful job without wanting to take over. It also means that we can initiate debate and promote activity around particular issues with much more confidence than in the past. We don't have to spend quite so much time sitting at the end of a 'phone waiting for the next call. To a limited degree, we can express our own view of what the main issues are, or should be. And we can express our own view of what people should be doing about it.

So there is, quite properly, a tension in our work between serving too uncritically and pushing too forcefully. What stops us getting too puffed up with our own importance is the control exercised by the members — by the groups and individuals who subscribe. In the end, they exercise control by voting with their feet.

Looking for new ways to recover some old habits of popular organisation and struggle isn't really any of our business. This job belongs to the trade union member in the office and factory, the women on the housing estate and the young unemployed. Sooner or later, against all the odds, they will make it their business.

CHAPTER FIVE
A Report from the Unit for the Development of Alternative Products

Brian Lowe

In their Alternative Corporate Plan[1] the Lucas Aerospace Workers described their ideas for Socially Useful Products which might be manufactured by the company in place of armaments.

The problem they faced, however, was the need to develop these ideas from concepts into actual products which could be the basis of job protection and job creation. Their experience of manufacturing industry made them well aware of the difficulties of converting ideas into viable products.

The establishment of the Centre for Alternative Industrial and Technological Systems, CAITS, made a valuable contribution to the solution of some of these problems. A number of projects were developed, notably the Road-Rail vehicle. Such work was restricted, however, by the lack of the substantial resources which were required.

Then in 1980, after considerable discussion of how to develop and extend this work, the need for further help was recognised by the Barrow & Geraldine S. Cadbury Trust. They offered financial support to establish a centre where the technical viability of the products outlined in the Corporate Plan might be more thoroughly investigated. As with CAITS, it was considered important to establish a partnership with an institution of higher education for the purpose of forming such a Centre. After several unfruitful negotiations with a variety of institutions, agreement was reached with the Governors of the Coventry (Lanchester) Polytechnic.[1] The Unit for the Development of Alternative Products (UDAP), was established in September 1981 as an integral part of the Department of Combined Engineering.

Early Stages

The initial design of the Unit was for two workers: a co-ordinator and a development engineer. The policies and direction of the Unit was the responsibility of the Steering

Committee consisting of equal numbers of representatives from the Combine and the Polytechnic. The execution of those policies and the day to day operation of the Unit was the responsibility of the staff. The expressed aim of the Unit was to design and develop to the point of production a range of items which are considered to fulfil socially useful criteria rather than merely meet a market need. It was hoped that such products might, in addition to reducing redundancy, actually be the means of creating new jobs. It was also considered that methods of production which would provide satisfying work was as important as the products themselves.

Work began in September 1981, the objective being

"to demonstrate the technical feasibility of a range of alternative socially useful products".

The ideas for such products came from a variety of sources. The work was organised by initiating projects (for students on a degree course in Design) on a number of product development topics. The Unit members undertook the co-ordination of the wide range of product development programmes involved.

The Corporate Plan ideas of the Lucas workers resulted in a number of projects: final drive design and investigation of the tyre characteristics of the Road-Rail vehicle; a design feasibility study of lightweight portable kidney machines; and the testing of a novel design of windmill proposed by Professor Rosenbrock of the University of Manchester's Institute of Science and Technology (UMIST).

As a complement to these ideas, the Department of Combined Engineering proposed a range of project work for the Unit, in particular the development of an Electric City Car intended as a 'fuel economic', low pollutant vehicle for use in urban areas. The engineering of the vehicle had been carried out as a series of individual and group projects over the previous three years. The body design and development had been undertaken by a student from the Department of Industrial Design. Until the arrival of UDAP the project had been viewed as an academic exercise; it was now seen to be a potential product and development activity assumed a new urgency. The relationship with the Department of Industrial Design was revitalised and students from that Department also began to take on project work which was promoted by the Unit.

As well as ideas from both constituent parties it was agreed during initial discussions that there should be one major jointly formulated project — a core project undertaken by the Unit. The decision on this proposal was made by the Steering

Committee which took the idea of hybrid power from the Corporate Plan and the electric city vehicle from the Department and blended them into the Hybrid Vehicle. The aim was to produce a vehicle suitable for urban operation which would combine the low fuel consumption and the environment-friendly features of the electric vehicle with the extended range and flexibility which the internal combustion engine offered. The development vehicle will be based on a light commercial chassis developed as a kit-built vehicle based on British Leyland (BL) Mini technology. Production vehicles will be designed as passenger carrying and commercial variants. Compared with the products of the large motor manufacturers the market for the hybrid vehicle will be small. The design takes this into account; it is best suited to low capital investment and labour intensive production methods. It will be reliable and durable and it will be built by people with the customer in mind.

During this first stage of activity other product ideas came out of contacts made with the community. Projects were promoted as part of a job creation project, which was being supported by one of the Combine members. An Industrial Design student developed a range of aids for disabled people. These included a 'papoose' for carrying older handicapped children, a shopping trolley which converted to a seat for older and infirm users, and a bathing aid for severely handicapped children. The work of exploring ideas for alternative products by means of student project activity has continued and grown. Typically a hundred students overall may be involved in any given academic year.

UDAP and the West Midlands: Industrial Initiatives

Soon after the foundation of UDAP, however, the Unit underwent a significant change. Councillors from the Economic Development Committee of the West Midlands County Council saw the possibility of the Unit contributing to their general policy of re-energising the declining economy of the region. They had already made several initiatives, including the establishment of an Enterprise Board and three Co-operative Development Agencies (CDAs), which aimed to help both medium/small size companies to survive and to support the creation of new forms of working ventures.

UDAP was seen as a source of technical support for those co-operative ventures and small enterprises which might require it. The method of utilising student project work was obviously inappropriate because of the long timescales involved. This major difficulty was overcome by the West Midlands County Council by a provision of funding which allowed the employment of a further three engineers and a part-time clerical assistant. The people appointed came from a variety of backgrounds and experience; (mechanical, electronics, production) engineering and from industrial design. The aim was to provide the widest base possible of technical support in order to assist organisations throughout a product development activity.

The nature of the work of the Unit changed and the people approaching the Unit began to fall into two broad categories: first, those who wanted help with the development of their own ideas for potential products and, second, those who had particular skills and were searching for ideas which would be the means of utilising them.

Some Examples

Jean was referred to the Unit by the Coventry Co-operative Development Agency to seek help with the development of a product with which she hoped to start a small enterprise. She wanted to produce an up-to-date version of a 'haybox'. This device allows a pot of food, after being brought to the boil and placed in a box surrounded by hay (which acts as an insulator) to continue cooking slowly without the need for any additional heat. Jean thought that this technique might now be useful as an energy saving device particularly for elderly people and those on low incomes. Her idea was to replace the hay with a modern, hygienic material.

The work was done by Jean with support, materials and facilities made available for her to learn the techniques and processes necessary to determine the best material for the job. She was also given assistance with the design of the container. The traditional rigid box was replaced by a stain resistant woven material both for economy and to employ her own skills. Finally, the Unit was able to get help with product assessment. The Catering Department of the student hall of residence at the Polytechnic used the device to cook a variety of dishes and produced a comprehensive report on their findings. This report was used as technical information in the preparation of a feasibility report which in turn was used to gain the financial support to launch the manufacturing and selling operation.

Mike, on the other hand, was a redundant machine tool skilled fitter who wanted to work for himself or in a co-operative enterprise but had no firm idea about potential products. A range of possibilities were discussed with him and a specific product emerged that fitted his skills and interests. This particular idea originated from a member of the academic staff who had worked with Oxfam whilst on a short sabbatical leave investigating their transport operations. One aspect of this was the movement of very large quantities of waste rags, the low density of which meant that a lorry with a load capacity of twenty tons could only carry four tons because of its bulk. A requirement was identified for some device which could compress the rags into more compact packages and thus allow more efficient use of the transport.

A member of the Unit worked with Mike on the initial design and he produced the first prototype. When this was complete it was presented to the Oxfam directorate and was then field-tested with the assistance of voluntary staff of three local Oxfam shops. The outcome of these tests has resulted in a changed specification required by Oxfam and further prototype development is now anticipated.

This one product will clearly not provide a continuing source of work for Mike and others, but it is intended to form the basis of a good start-up activity for an engineering enterprise to which further products may be added in time.

UDAP and the West Midlands: Coventry Workshop

Meanwhile the Unit has been establishing a working relationship with the local trade union and community resource unit — the Coventry Workshop. The Workshop had been active in assisting a range of local community groups in Coventry for some years before the foundation of UDAP and the CDAs. They have acted as a resource centre for local trade unions, residents' associations and community action groups. UDAP was seen to be a way of extending those resources to cover scientific and technical aspects. From this context, and via the Coventry Trades Council, a local branch of the Transport and General Workers' Union approached the Unit for assistance. The workers came from a wholesale food distribution company. Although the immediate future of the firm, and the jobs of the workers, appeared to be secure, the branch officials had begun to consider possible alternatives which might be necessary in more difficult times ahead. Discussions between the branch officials and UDAP produced a range of potential alternative company structures and operational methods which might be a viable basis for future work should the current situation deteriorate seriously. This process can be seen to have been directly influenced by the model established by the Lucas workers and their development of the Alternative Corporate Plan.

Tenants' associations were also introduced to the Unit by the Workshop. One such group consisted of tenants from a private housing association seeking help with establishing the causes of dampness which were occurring in members' homes because of structural defects, and as a result of condensation. The initial work was carried out by a volunteer worker in the Unit who offered to help during the summer vacation from his graduate engineering course at Warwick University.[2] The main work was then carried out by a full-time member of UDAP with specialist assistance from academic staff of the Polytechnic. The resulting report[3] was then used as the basis of negotiation between the tenants and the Housing Association. The outcome was extremely satisfactory, as all of the recommendations presented were accepted by the Association and corrective action is currently underway improving these homes to the benefit of the tenants.

Another tenants' association, this time in a council housing estate, but also specifically concerned with problems of health connected with dampness in homes, was helped with a computer analysis of a questionnaire which had been completed by a majority of tenants on the estate. Once again a volunteer worker was involved; a student from a local sixth-form college working with the Unit for the summer vacation. A dedicated analysis programme was produced and instruction given in how to use it. Members of the association were then given use of Polytechnic micro-computers to complete their analysis, the results of which were to be used in a submission to the local authority.

A spin-off from this last piece of work was that one member of the tenants' group expressed interest in investigating the use of bricks made from recycled newspaper as a domestic fuel. Again facilities were organised within the Polytechnic for standard testing.

It soon became clear that a commercial operation was not viable and investigations continued into the possibility of producing the bricks in a community workshop for free distribution to pensioners and other low income families. Although process methods had soon been defined the fuel would not be granted a smokeless classification — essential if it were to be used in an urban environment — and development work was halted. The details are documented in a UDAP report.[4]

Then, in 1982, British Aerospace announced the closure (over six months) of their site at Bitteswell in Leicestershire, with the loss of more than 1,000 jobs. Although the factory was some 15 miles from the centre of Coventry the majority of the workforce lived in the West Midlands and few of them were able to find alternative employment. Using existing trade union structures they began to discuss their reactions to the closure and formulate ideas for possible alternatives. Aided by Coventry Workshop, they made a decision to stay together and attempt to create work for themselves. Thus, the Bitteswell Employment Alliance was founded with more than 250 members as a cooperative enterprise based on the skills of the membership. UDAP then became involved assisting in identifying and evaluating ideas for a diverse range of products and services on which they might found their enterprise. The ideas for such products came from a variety of sources, in particular a skill audit of the members was carried out and, at a series of general meetings, ideas for potential products and services were discussed. A management committee was elected and five project groups were formed with the intention of following up specific ideas. At this point it was clear that UDAP must now reorganise its own methods of working in order to respond to the emerging needs of the Alliance. This was done by associating one UDAP worker with each of the Product Groups: Utility Transport, Aids for Disabled, Energy, Leisure products and Electrical products.

The first of these groups sought to use their skills to produce custom made van bodies for existing commercial chassis. While investigating such possibilities their attention was drawn to a kit-form vehicle produced by a well established small company. In addition to producing custom bodies this presented the opportunity to supply the kits and provide assistance with the construction of the vehicles. Space was provided for the building of the first prototype within the Polytechnic and student project work was undertaken on the initial design of a range of alternative bodies.

The 'Aids for Disabled' group sought to develop a range of products designed to help people with a variety of disabilities. Several of these ideas came from students of the Department of Industrial Design. The Unit was again able to help with provision of space and facilities for making prototypes, assisted with the selection of tools and materials and made available the library and other reference sources. As with 'Utility Vehicles' this group has since moved to their own premises to complete the development work. The experience of working with such a large group as the Bitteswell Employment Alliance has resulted in the Unit examining closely its own methods of operation and caused the three support agencies to look more critically at the ways in which they worked together. Regular and structured tripartite meetings improved the overall efficiency of the three agencies in their relationship with the Alliance and made their work more effective. Each was beginning to learn more about the nature of the problems and how to attempt to solve them.

Difficulties, Successes

In each of these projects difficulties have arisen, some associated with particular projects, others recurring from project to project. Two major issues stand in the way of community groups or other workers who are contemplating these initiatives. Firstly, they need to develop viable products whose manufacture is appropriate to the skills and interests of the workers concerned, and secondly the need for effective marketing once production has been established. UDAP has attempted to support the first of these needs.

Market research and sales promotion, however, present a different set of problems. The market assessment of a product, the preparation of a production and marketing strategy and the organising of outlets are vital activities which are extremely time consuming and require particular skills which were not available from within UDAP nor from within the other existing support groups. Consultants hired at great expense did not appear able to do a satisfactory job because they did not seem to appreciate the social criteria which were being applied.

To combat these problems the Unit has sought additional financial assistance to establish an independent marketing unit which might support job creation initiatives based on socially useful production.

The nature of the work of the Unit and the way in which it operates has evolved as the many problems encountered by working with the numerous groups involved have had to be tackled. These are problems concerning new relationships, new ways of working, breaking down demarcation lines, overcoming inhibition of using academic facilities, imposition of deadlines and planning, personality conflicts, restricted facilities and workspace, low levels of funding and finance and the need for communication and organisational development in parallel with the technical tasks. The original relatively simple aims of establishing the technical feasibility of alternative products has widened to encompass a much broader activity. The Unit has now become absorbed into and became a distinct but constituent part of the popular planning movement.

In contrast to these difficulties the work overall has registered a number of successes. First, there has been the demonstration that it is possible for individuals and groups from within the local community to make constructive use of the wealth of resources which exists within the Polytechnic. This in turn has helped to re-emphasise the publicly accountable nature of such institutions. Second, there has been the more obvious and direct success of contributing to the creation of jobs such as those connected with the utility transport group of the Bitteswell Employment Alliance. Thirdly, the Unit has proved to be the model for other endeavours intended to support alternative production. UDAP-like agencies are planned for Sheffield, Nottingham, Leicester, London and other localities.

Conclusion

The arguments put forward by the Lucas Combine in 1976 and subsequently to promote their Corporate Plan concept now have more relevance than ever before. Structural unemployment, especially in manufacturing industry, together with the deepening energy crisis, cry out for alternative ways of employing people. We need to use broader criteria than exchange value to determine product choice. The concept of meeting the needs of the 'Social Market' and how best this can be organised by society in a more direct manner must be developed in order to get this activity recognised as a vital ingredient in the wealth creation process.

The central feature of socially useful production is the development of ideas and organisational forms that encourage involvement, generate self confidence and release new found or rediscovered skills during the examination of how productive resources should be used to meet social needs. Initiatives promoting socially useful production must, in turn, be extremely responsible and very supportive *throughout the complete process* if working people are to successfully take on the tasks and challenges of responding with alternative plans.

At a time when public expenditure cuts coincide with massive sums of money being paid out on unemployment benefits, redundancy payments and social security benefits, this approach to challenging apparently mindless redundancy, and directing energy and demands into socially useful production, is a serious one regarding both the social and economic problems which affect all sections of the community.

References

1. Wainwright and Elliot, *The Lucas Plan*. Allison and Busby, London, 1982.
2. Chapman, A., 'Dampness and Housing'. UDAP, October 1982.
3. Irving, B., 'Investigation of eleven houses suffering from dampness in the Coventry area', UDAP, March 1983.
4. Irving, B., 'Paper Briquettes as a Domestic Fuel', UDAP, April 1983.

VOICES

Women and Labour and the Alternative Economic Strategy

Women . . . "The crucial consideration for them is not availability of work, but what kind of work they do, how much of their time they spend on it, how much they get paid for it (if anything), and the degree of their economic dependence or control. The AES does not address itself to such matters . . . If women had power to assert their own experience, as men have, we might develop a different approach, one with a double axis: reproduction and production . . . When we have decided on the best way of caring for our children and the most effective means of supporting them; when we have resolved to re-allocate labour and wealth within the family; and when we have worked out how best to restructure paid employment and improve state services, *then* is the time to decide how to pay for what we need."

Anna Coote, The AES: a new starting point. *New Socialist* Nov/Dec 1981, and Bea Campbell, who also contributed to this article.

Labour's published plan for jobs

- Expansion for jobs
- Planning for industrial recovery
- Fair trade and competitive pound
- Price controls to check inflation
- National economic assessment
- An equal right to work
- Making money for Britain
- The right to control our lives
- International co-operation

So where is socially useful production as:

- Socially useful work?
- Ideas of change of production for social use?
- Assessment of products for their social use?
- Recognition of unpaid labour in the home?
- Ecologically sound investment?
- Economic co-operation in principled world development?
- Encouragement of cultural autonomy and socially useful cultural production?
- Encouragement of co-operative forms of organisation?
- Mechanisms for popular planning?
- A policy on arms conversion?

Lucas Combine on Labour

"We got every encouragement, short of actual help" — Lucas Steward on the Labour Government.

Workers' Plans

"The most publicised aspect of such plans is the proposal for 'socially useful' production — i.e. alternative products to those for which there is no longer a market. The problem is that if such products are intended for sale to the public sector (like kidney machines) then the argument is really about the level and allocation of public spending. If the products are intended for private markets or governments overseas and they can be sold at a profit, then the alternative plan is reduced to a critique — which may well be justified but is hardly radical — of capitalist market research. If they can only be sold at a loss then subsidy in some form is necessary and this demands some form of public intervention. Workers' Plans are not therefore an *alternative* to state intervention and the AES."

Conference of Socialist Economists

"What amount of wealth we should produce if we are all working cheerfully at producing the things that we all genuinely want; if all the intelligence, all the inventive power, all the inherited skill of handicraft, all the keen wit and insight, all the healthy bodily strength were engaged in doing this and nothing else, what a pile of wealth we should have! How would poverty be a word whose meaning we should have forgotten! Believe me, there is nothing but the curse of inequality which forbids this."

William Morris

"That, as soon as practicable, this Society shall proceed to arrange the powers of production, distribution, education and government, or in other words, to establish a self-supporting home colony of united interests, or assist other societies in establishing such colonies."

Rochdale Pioneers, *Statement of Objects,* 1844

PART TWO

Extending the Politics

CHAPTER SIX
Not My Type — Choices in Technology and Organisation for Printing
Cynthia Cockburn

Work can be a torture or a pleasure; it can diminish the worker or it can enable growth and learning. These are big issues; they profoundly affect the individual's life experience. The right to a satisfying working life is probably as fundamental as the right to food and shelter. So it matters a good deal how much we can make those eight hours a day serve our own interests as well as those of an employer.

Workplaces are continually subject to technical change and often the introduction of new machinery and ways of doing things has the purpose of de-skilling, limiting the initiative of the worker and reducing the cost to the employer of human labour. But this is not always achieved so simply. Peoples' relationship to actual technological hardware is a complex one and depends very much on who designed the equipment and for what purpose; and who sets people to work on it and how.

There is a complicated two-way interaction between the relations involved in different ways of organising work and the relations involved in using different levels and types of technology. Capitalist relations of work are exploitative in principle but can be modified in certain real life situations. Co-operative relations of work are non-exploitative in principle but, in practice, the need to survive in a hard competitive world can lead to harmful decisions about technology. Besides, the technology commercially available severely limits choice.

The Printing Industry

The story of typesetting for print illustrates some of these complexities. Type used to be set in metal — specifically, in lead alloy. The skilled men who did the work of composition had succeeded, over the decades, by means of thorough trade union organisation, in limiting the extent to which their capitalist employers were free to make hay with their labour power. They had organised a pre-entry closed shop, and kept a tight control on apprenticeship and on the actual organisation of work. As a result, wages in printing crafts ranged from the merely decent to the astronomical.

In the last 20 years, lead has been dispensed with. Electronic and photographic principles have been applied in systems of great elegance and efficiency that make the typesetting process now very simple and very fast. This technology has been developed quite purposefully by those firms that saw a market among print employers who had long wanted to get rid of their craftsmen. Now, in theory, any typist, male or female, can be trained for typesetting in a few days.

In practice, of course, the trade union organisation has not proved so easy to dislodge. There is not a national newspaper organisation in Britain that yet uses the new electronic composing systems as they are designed to be used. In none have the unions allowed the worker to be entirely subordinated to the logic of the system. In the USA, however, where the union was less powerful, the old craft control has gone by the board. Many newspaper typesetters are now women.

On the other hand, the restructuring of the printing industry and print workforce over the last 20 years, combined with the advent of this new technology, have had the contradictory effect of making it more possible for small independent typesetting outfits to spring up. A few of these are co-operatives, and in both, again, women may be found at the keyboards.

Two Short Stories

I want to describe two enterprises and their technologies, to contrast their purpose, and their organisation and chosen technology. One is a large newspaper group operating within the normal capitalist market economy, using an advanced system of electronic typesetting to the peak of its potential. The other is a woman's typesetting co-op with a very different product, different organisation and different equipment. If the two at times sound like caricatures, it is worth remembering that it is life, not literature, that produces such extremes.

The Daily News

The newspaper group we can call *The Daily News*, and its equipment the *Tronic-Type* system. *Tronic-Type* is not any one make, nor is *The Daily News* any one newspaper house. The picture is a composite, based on knowledge of several systems marketed today and on the cherished hopes and intentions of managers and technical specialists I have interviewed in four newspaper firms.

The heart of the *Tronic-Type* system of newspaper production, which as a whole cost its owners £5 million, is a powerful computer. Apart from its computational facility, this computer is, most importantly, the very capacious memory of the system. In it must be stored not only all the articles and reports published from day to day in *The Daily News* and its sister titles, but such matter as stocks and share prices, football league data and horse racing 'form', all continually updated. It has to be understood however that this is no longer just a system for composing type. *Tronic-Type* is an integrated editorial/composing/advertising/accounting system. Therefore the memory also holds the text of all advertisements placed in the papers, information on the credit-worthiness of advertisers, and details of their accounts.

On line to the central computer are a score of mini-computers. Each is the focus of four video display terminals, and serves as their intelligence. Each VDT has a screen on which text may be represented, and a keyboard with the normal typewriter alphabet and some additional keys with which to instruct the computer.

From Beating Hearts to Pacemakers

The heart of type production in an old-style newspaper such as *The Daily News* was ten years previously, had been a large team of hot-metal compositors. The heart has shifted in the new system. It is not comps at all, but journalists — both reporters and editors. Journalists, instead of writing with biro and paper, now have their VDTs. Stories are written direct onto the screen, amended to the reporter's satisfaction and stored in the computer memory. The sub-editor can call up a 'menu' of those stories ready for the next edition, call any one of them onto his* screen by pressing a few keys, read it, amend it, fit it for size (the computer telling him how many lines at a given measure it will make) and without further ado 'send' it to be set as type.

The next item of equipment that comes into play is the photosetter. Responding to the output demands of the many keyboards, it produces the characters and words on a cathode ray tube and finally on photographic bromide paper, looking like finished text in black on white. In the process of doing this, it 'digitises' each character of the alphabet as it encounters it. Say

---

*This is not sexist usage. It reflects the facts: owners, managers, editors, reporters and printers in newspapers are almost 100 per cent male.

a 't' is to be produced. The photosetter's computer specifies the tiny dots that will combine to form a 't' of the size and slant, the thickness and style, that have been specified. The photosetter works with tremendous rapidity. It sets thousands of characters per second. It is one of those clever machines that has taken into itself the know-how of generations of craftsmen and created an unskilled job: photosetter operation amounts to little more than feeding in occasional new rolls of bromide paper and tearing off the set text as the long galleys spew out.

Meanwhile, much of the raw material that eventually gets worked into articles for the newspaper is communicated to the news desk from the outside world electronically. Formerly printed out on a 'telex', this is now fed direct into the computer memory and may be edited in the same manner as any other story.

No Loose Ends in this Organisation

The reading public sometimes forgets that newspapers, even national newspapers, are as much advertising as news media. Adverts come to the paper by phone or by mail. The new electronic system offers tremendous advantages to the newspaper publisher in dealing with adverts. The advert typist is nearly always a women — commonly diminished in the nickname 'tele-ad girl'. She has her own VDT. When she receives a call from an advertiser, she enters the company or individual name on the keyboard and immediately receives feedback in the shape of a credit clearance or credit 'blacking' from the computer. The typist then takes down details of the ad, tapping on her keyboard, viewing on her screen. The computer's capability to prefigure the size of type and length of line enables her to give the advertiser an accurate quote on lineage and cost. If she sees a single word or two on the ultimate line she can advise the advertiser to add a word or two more. The accounts department's records are automatically brought up to date, the advertiser debited with the cost, an invoice printed out for mailing. Ads can be stored and easily updated for a further edition, automatically killed when they have run their time. The cost accountants can receive an instantaneous and accurate assessment of the advertising revenue of any day's edition. And finally, the advert copy, as typed by the tele-ad typist, can directly activate the photosetter.

Meanwhile, however, some copy does still have to be set by the few remaining compositors. Outside contributors to *The Daily News*, who do not have the benefit of an on-line terminal, still

send in their copy as typescript for re-setting. So there remain a
few 'comps', the rump of the *News*'s once sizeable composing
room, where the entire newspaper was set in molten lead.
Because the *Tronic-Type* system at *The News* is used by the
employers for 'direct entry' by journalists, most of the material
by-passing the comps, the trade union has blacked the firm. The
comps here are therefore, in union terms, scabs.

Skills, Quality and Control

These comps, now more correctly called keyboard operators, are
the only workers at *The Daily News* who spend all their day at a
keyboard, setting text. Their job therefore bears closer
examination. The *Tronic-Type* system has had a deleterious
effect on the labour process. The operators, unlike the former
comps, do not get little breaks in the job, walking about
collecting and delivering copy. They no longer have the power to
decide for each line where to end and move to the next, how to
break any words that need a hyphen. All this is now done for
them by the computer. They do not select their measure, type
face and type size. Indeed they may never know what style they
are working in, unless they can decipher the format code that
they are required to blindly copy. The operators set text in a
continual stream. Since speed is the aim, they are not
encouraged to look at their own work on the screen and make
corrections, but to tap uninterruptedly, leaving it to the proof
reader to make amendments. All sense of pride in a 'clean' job is
gone. Since operators no longer even see their output, they do
not know how much they have set or how fast and well. It is, as
many of them are quick to say, a 'battery hen' job.

The *Tronic-Type* system described here is physically like an
octopus, with many out-reaching tentacles. It models the
hierarchical, centralised nature of a large-scale newspaper
operation in a capitalist world. The managers, line managers,
financial managers, senior executives, they too have their VDTs
and on them they can call for reports on the flow of work, check
the performance of their departments, count the output of
individuals. They can send commands that flash up on workers'
screens. They and their technical experts alone have the
overview and the initiative that can adapt the software and
hardware to yet more productivity and more effective control of
production. The counter-vailing power that used to reside in the
deft hand of the craftsman has been neutralised by a
combination of equipment and re-organisation.

Text Type Ltd.

Let's now move away from *The Daily News*, round to the backstreets and the small premises of a woman's co-operative called *Text Type Ltd*. The co-op is imaginary, but is based on the experience of a real one.

The aim of work organisation at *Text Type Ltd.* is that every woman typesetter has as much control over what she does, as much chance to develop her skill and take an interest in her job, as is compatible with producing enough to enable the firm to prosper. The challenge was to select from essentially capitalist technolgy a system that could serve, or at least not subvert, this end.

Small, Cheap and Useful

The system they chose we can call *Wordmaker I*. The co-op purchased six stand-alone units, not much bigger than desks, all identical. Each cost around £16,000. Every *Wordmaker I* unit has a keyboard and screen. In this they do not differ from the VDTs of the *Tronic-Type* in use at *The News*. Where the difference lies is in the relation of this unit to the system's memory and to its output unit. In the *Wordmaker I* system this is all within the physical confines of the small unit at which the typesetter sits, and is under her direct control and that of no one else. There is no unskilled ancillary 'photosetter operator' job here. Up to her left, within reach of her hand, is a rack containing a series of floppy discs. Each of these is equivalent to a file in an old-style document filing cabinet.

Convivial Jobbing Work

This little typesetting firm has many regular jobs. One, for instance, is setting a monthly community newspaper, *The Street Crier*. This newspaper has its own floppy disc. All the material set for its successive editions is held here for some months after publication. Each operator keeps by her all the discs such as this one that represent her regular responsibility. She deals with the clients, she knows their needs and is often in a position to suggest improvements in style or procedure. The client too can see and understand the equipment and the production process. It can be 'demystified' so as to give the client a sense of control too, and improve relations between client and typesetter.

The *Wordmaker*'s output unit is a small photosetter immediately adjacent to the keyboard and screen unit. It can contain any two of a variety of type founts (an alphabet in a particular style). These founts take the physical shape of a strip of film around half a metre in length and five centimetres wide, containing the upper and lower case letters of the alphabet and some additional characters in light, medium, italic and bold forms.

How She Works

To start setting work on a new edition of *The Street Crier*, the typesetter opens the photosetter apparatus, removes the fount she has been using and replaces it with the one demanded by the new job. She also inserts into the front of the unit, above the keyboard, the appropriate 'spacing card'. This is required because different styles of type face involve characters of different width. The card instructs the photosetter to advance the appropriate distance to accommodate the characters of the style being used.

The typesetter now withdraws the appropriate floppy disc from its rack and positions it in the unit. She takes her place at the keyboard and makes a number of decisions, which she transmits to the unit's memory. She has already chosen the type style. Now she chooses the line measure, the line spacing, the letter spacing and the type size, that seem to her appropriate or which have been specified by the client. She tells the machine to set 'ragged' or 'justified' or 'centred'. These instructions, once transmitted to memory, may be given a 'format code', so that the entire set may be reactivated by simply depressing a couple of keys on any future occasion. She herself chooses the code tag.

In a sense, the typesetter builds up a library of tricks that she can call on speedily, that she alone knows her way around. *Text Type Ltd.* have made a collective decision that the line ends and word breaks will not be done by computer but will remain at the discretion of the typesetter herself. This both improves the quality of the work and adds to the interest of the job. The worker can however build up her own dictionary, on disc, of certain words that occur frequently in a job, indicating where they should be broken. She can even institute summary codes that will reproduce whole phrases that occur over and over again in a text, so avoiding the need to type them every time.

An indicator on the screen informs the typesetter how many lines she has set, and after a given number she presses the 'set' button and the photosetter can be heard spinning into action beside her, photographing the stored text, character by character, onto bromide film. Meanwhile she continues with her setting. Eventually she processes and sees her finished product.

The bromide galley is now sent back to the client for approval and alterations and corrections are marked on. The proofs return to the woman who set them, so that she herself may have the satisfaction of completing and perfecting the job she started. She inserts *The Street Crier* disc once more, asks the computer to 'search' for the sequence of words in the text that require correction. She superimposes the video's cursor on the characters to be replaced and retypes them, thus replacing the old file with a correct version.

At *Text Type Ltd.* the women specialise in subjects and forms of setting that interest them. One woman who happens to have a degree in literature often chooses to set books. Another is building up a special expertise in scientific and mathematical work, learning to construct equations and even to build new characters out of combinations of existing ones. This learning process is embodied in her files, the floppy discs of past work, which speed and facilitate present work.

Control: Resistance and Constraints

The aim of the owner of a large national newspaper like *The Daily News*, what he wants from his production system, is control. Specifically he wants his managers to be able to control the flow of work and the deployment and use of his employees. Rupert Murdoch, when he bought *The Times* and *The Sunday Times*, to add to *The Sun* and the rest of his news empire, inherited a battle between management and craftsmen over the 'proper' use of a sophisticated computerised composition system. Even today, three years after his purchase, Murdoch is nowhere near achieving the goal of a direct-entry system such as I have described earlier in this chapter. The craftsmen know their interests and are resisting with all their organised might.

The aim of a women's co-op, by contrast, is to empower its members. But that goal, too, is difficult to achieve. The class relations that result in a struggle on the shop floor of a newspaper can't altogether be evaded even in a co-op. *Text Type Ltd.* operates in a capitalist market. If clients have learned to expect a wide choice of type faces, for instance, and can get it from other firms, then *Text Type* may be forced to buy in technology that prioritises the range of type faces rather than operator-control. Besides, there are some kinds of work that, for both technical and organisation reasons, *Text Type* has to turn down. The firms that design and produce the equipment are continually predicting the big markets, the dominant trends — they are not interested in *Text Type Ltd.* as a client.

The thrust is to more and more push-button operation because that is what a capitalist employer wants. *Text Type Ltd.* enter the scene only after design decisions have been made: they must just take what is on offer. As it happens, the simple stand-alone system described as *Wordmaker I* was only a temporary stage in the technology's development. It has now gone out of production. When the women have to replace their worn-out units they will have no choice but to go 'up technology'. They will be obliged to buy a system with a centralised computer and photosetter units to which several keyboards are on-line. It is undeniably more 'sensible' and 'efficient', but they feel they will lose that intimate relationship they have with their machines today. The co-op feel they are being pushed towards more business-minded decisions and a less human way of using the technology.

To Sum Up

What we have seen here is not only two modes of production and two contrasted examples of technology. It is also two very different kinds of product: a national newspaper and jobbing work, which make different organisational demands. However, it is not only newspapers that are highly routinised. Many general trade typesetting houses are operated on high-productivity lines too, with an advanced degree of division of labour and de-skilled operation.

A woman working in a printshop similar to *Text Type Ltd.* described the difference between the two ways of work in this way. "We have organised things so that we can take an interest in the work and take responsibility for it. People say to me 'how can an intelligent person like you sit at a keyboard all day?' But I spend my day *reading* as I set, and understanding what I read. Women sometimes come to us after working in trade typesetting houses. It's horrifying. They have no idea what they have been setting, no idea what measure or type they use. They have become like wooden people".

Nothing is absolutely given in the technology. Nothing is absolutely given in a capitalist economy or in a patriarchal society. Nor is the technology we have simply a mirror of the mode of production and the sex and gender system that gives rise to it. There are always some products thrown up in each new wave of technology, and some opportunities emerging from each new restructuring of work, that can be turned to workers' and women's advantage. Small offset presses, photocopying, electronic stencil-cutting have all been seized on to furnish community and women's presses.

The overthrow of craft control and apprenticeship has opened up training and work for women from which they were excluded before. But the dominant tendencies in both capitalist technology and capitalist labour processes push against worker satisfaction and against working class and women's control. We have no choice but to think on our feet.

A MODERN UTOPIA?

1. The Festival of Britain — Vision for a modern Britain?

Although a national event, rather than a metropolitan one, the Festival of Britain marked the centenary of the Great Exhibition of 1851. It was a mixture of ad hoc local activities, highly planned exhibits, tradition and modern innovation. The Festival's focal point was in London on the South Bank of the Thames. As a spectacle, and encounter, the event could be visited as — a good day out for the re-united, or newly formed, family; as a means to experience the 'wonders' of science and technology; and as a chance to sample a modern built environment. However, we should understand both the South Bank and the Festival generally as very contradictory in conception and reception. It could be seen to span objectives which: set out to counter the drabness of the post war period by its colour and fun; presented elements of a social democratic vision by its content and media descriptions; and gave a focus to stimulate production and consumption.

While the Festival had utopian elements these were never unified into a clear and agreed vision. As a project of the post war Labour Government it came late in their period of office, too late to revitalize their jaded popularity. Furthermore, it never became bonded into that popular vision which propelled the Government into office. Such a failure showed that this political enterprise overlooked the power of pleasure and desire to drive a demand for an elaborated and visualised future. This lesson has still to be learned by the Labour Party.

2. Mondragon — A modern Utopia?

Mondragon is a small town in the Basque country of Spain, about 30 miles from Bilbao. Over the last twenty years the town has become internationally known as a centre of producer co-operatives. The first one was formed in 1956. Currently there are about sixty co-ops with a combined workforce numbering over 13,000. Collectively, they have a turnover of something in the order of £200m. Within this community of interest the co-operative ethic has generated a very comprehensive support structure. This includes a bank, the Caja Laboral Popular, schools, a college of technology, a research centre, and housing, consumer and agricultural co-operatives. Mondragon also has a co-operative which handles social security for the entire complex.

The setting for the growth of this co-operative experiment was a region which had been economically devastated by war and politically and culturally oppressed by Franco's regime. It therefore can be seen as a particular example of resistance, in an area with a political culture of resistance.

While the rise of Mondragon has resulted from the efforts of many, its history acknowledges a debt to one particular man — Jose Maria Arizmondi, an ex-republican soldier and prisoner who became a priest. On being given a mission by the church to work as a counsellor and advisor to young people in the Basque country, his response was to conserve and work towards material aid, especially with respect to education and co-operation. Thus his effort made a very significant contribution towards the creative climate out of which the project emerged.

Mondragon does not have the high idealism of many C18th and C19th Utopias. However, it does demonstrate the prospect of micro economic and social progress in what at least at the start was a hostile climate. Of such projects we do need to ask if they are a protetypic basis for the development of viable utopias.

Alastair Campbell *et al*, *Worker-Owners: The Mondragon Achievement* Anglo-German Foundation for the Study of Industrial Society 1977.

CHAPTER SEVEN
Worker Co-operatives in Wales: A Framework for Socially Useful Production?
Philip Cooke

Introduction

It is arguable that one of the earliest, most clearly thought through and practically applicable workers' plans for socially useful production was that published for the coal industry in 1911 by the Rhondda-based Unofficial Reform Committee as *The Miners' Next Step*. This document expressed its disillusion with conventional party political efforts to produce economic reform and put the syndicalist case for direct action in the sphere of production. It called for the socialisation of the coal mines, the development of a broadly-based Industrial Union within and beyond the mining industry, and, above all, for alternative forms of management or 'leadership' of both trade unions and the industries which were the basis for their organisation. Leaders were seen as corruptible, having a vested interest in resisting change which might threaten their jobs. Thus the logic of this analysis was that

> "The men (sic) must retain control by having the final say in all negotiations in the ballot box, and leaders are to be reduced to ambassadors from the men to their employers. And here the argument takes off into different realms . . . (the union) was not only in a position to dictate the men's conditions of work, but further . . . it presented the most direct and desirable route towards total control. Industrial unionism as a path to workers' control did not seem, to many, impossibly utopian in these conditions".[1]

The story of how this dream was subverted, so that a hierarchical form of control came to dominate the South Wales and other coalfields after nationalisation in 1947, has yet to be fully told. Suffice it to say at this point that the form of ownership of productive means that post-war nationalisation of coal and other basic industries took, emasculated both the trades unions and the workers in the industries in question. So much so that the source of energy 'from below', whose impetus took vast industries out of private hands, was never again to be directed towards re-thinking the methods of organisation and control in their industry. Coal and steel, the core industries of South Wales until 1979, are good examples of the way in which state management of productive enterprise, no less than private management, channels the creative and radical strands of thought on behalf of organised labour into the narrow economism of wage-bargaining.

Wales as a whole, and South Wales especially, has placed an enormous amount of faith in traditional Labourist solutions to its economic and social problems. The responsibility for re-establishing the economic base has been delegated to state functionaries who share precisely similar characteristics to those 'leaders' which the Unofficial Reform Committee castigated so severely in 1911. Their reluctance to face the prospects of change resulted in supposedly publicly-owned corporations being run by the same expropriated managers of failed private industry. The model of control was that of the Herbert Morrison-governed London County Council of the inter-war years, arid and soulless. The prime concern was with ensuring that compensation payments were paid out in time for the expropriated to catch the next speculative boom whether in South African minerals or London office blocks. The secondary concern was to ensure cheap inputs to private industry by controlling prices and starving pits and steelworks of investment. Some distance further down the list of priorities came the development of employment opportunities and markets for new products.

As a result of this dependence on state control and management of industry in Wales, initiatives to recapture the progressive impulse of *The Miners' Next Step* in non-statist ways have simply not been on the agenda. That is, until the Thatcher government pulled the props out from under the post-war edifice.

Socially Useful Production: Some Problems

Although many of the practical ideas and programmes which underlie the general description "socially useful production" are very old, it would be true to say that the difficulties of, particularly, the British economy in the 1970s culminating in the post-1979 industrial catastrophe, have stimulated a wider interest in the prospects for alternatives to production for profit on the market. The Workers' Plans movement, the CAITS experiments and the local responses from progressive county and district councils represent, in limited ways, the working out of the complex problems of translating abstract ideas into practical action. Yet, while it cannot be denied that the basic principles of the Lucas Plan, or even the slightly less ambitious Vickers Plan[2] have never yet approached implementation, it is clear from the kinds of initiatives taken by progressive local authorities that we are still a long way from establishing the means for socially useful production on any significant scale.

The most obvious limitation upon the practical implementation of the principles developed in workers' plans for socially useful production is financial. An example of the scale of the problem can be taken from the attempt by workers and sympathetic interests to retain steel-making in two different countries, Britain and the USA.

Financing Take-overs: Lack of Labour Generated Capital Investment

When the Consett steelworks in north-east England was threatened with closure and the loss of 4,000 jobs, the protest from the workforce stimulated at least some interests sympathetic to the problems of 'a new Jarrow of the 1980s' to explore the costs of taking over the works and running it privately, though not, for example, co-operatively. The British Steel Corporation's asking price was £100 million; the most that the consortium in question could assemble was £3 million. Private sector backing was not available; for ideological reasons the state was opposed to any funding, and the labour movement simply has not got the resources or means of accumulating or distributing them for such purposes. The steelworks closed and 4,000 were added to the unemployed.[3]

This experience paralleled almost exactly that of workers in the American steel town of Youngstown, Ohio, who were faced with the loss of 4,100 jobs in the Youngstown Sheet and Tube Co. in 1977, a prelude to the loss of over 9,000 steel jobs in a two-year period. A popular, community-led initiative quickly emerged to explore the feasibility of worker ownership of the mills. They enlisted the aid of the radical National Centre for Economic Alternatives who costed the plan. They concluded it was feasible provided £250 million was immediately made available for new equipment and a further £65 million was in hand as working capital. If the community could raise the smaller sum, the federal government would guarantee loans for the larger amount. However, the community could 'only' manage to raise £2 million, so the closure went ahead, and 4,000 jobs disappeared.[4]

Clearly, both these examples refer to job-loss on a very large scale, consequently it might be argued that it is unfair to use them as examples of how workers might buy out their failing industry. It might also be argued that as examples they are not necessarily true to the ideals of socially useful production. On the latter point, it is not unreasonable to use steel as an example of a socially useful product, for the simple reason that it is a basic input to a great deal of industrial production whether socially useful or aimed merely at private profit-making. As for the former point, if workers' plans for socially useful production are to be substantially more than a rhetorical device, this is a necessary indication of the scale of finance which has to be available, multiplied manyfold!

In Britain and elsewhere it has been the state which has provided the only alternative source of finance on this scale to that of the private money-market. As things stand, neither the state nor the private sector will supply resources on such a scale. Even if a government sympathetic to socially useful production were in power, such expenditure would have to be prioritised against other demands. Moreover, it would leave the recipients vulnerable to being cut off financially if there were a change of government. Basically, what is being said here is that the lack of independent labour-generated investment capital means that socially useful production cannot make a substantial impact other than as rhetoric or very small scale experimentation. If the real function of the movement towards socially useful production is to offer limited hope that alternatives are possible, then that is an honourable purpose but we must be clear that moving beyond that position requires new institutions capable of generating large sums of investment capital. Creating such institutions at the level of ideas is the next great task, though it should have been the first.

Marketing

The other, lesser problem which can be discussed here applies at whatever scale socially useful production is carried out. It is undoubtedly feasible for a small worker buy-out enterprise, funded adequately by a local enterprise board, to turn from producing parts for tanks or nuclear weapons to producing components for cheap heat-pumps, better braking systems or telechiric[5] devices. But marketing such products may well prove to be the most difficult, as well as the most important part of the process. The importance of marketing to large and medium corporations is demonstrated by their sensitivity to the need for marketing departments to be centred in or near capital cities.

This applies even where their research or production facilities are located more peripherally[6] and signifies that a great deal of inter-corporate buying and selling is highly centralised. Given that most social production will be diffused and small-scale, the need for a strong, organised marketing structure to be established is paramount.

No doubt there are other far-reaching as well as more practical problems associated with production for use. Space does not permit a full analysis, but one to which I will return in the next section concerns the co-operative mode of organisation. Problems of self-exploitation by the labour force, and difficulty regarding capital-formation are endemic here, and need to be resolved if socially useful production is to move beyond the level of the sweatshop.

The Wales Trade Union Congress and Worker Co-operatives

Wales has been extremely badly hit in the present recession. Job-loss on a massive scale occurred, in the steel industry especially, from the late 1970s. Between 1980 and 1983 the Wales TUC estimated that the direct and indirect effects of the Welsh steel crisis had resulted in the loss of over 50,000 jobs.[7] This specific job-loss was preceded by a 7.5 per cent loss of total employees in employment between 1976 and 1980, a figure worse by a full percentage point than that of Wales' two nearest rivals, the West Midlands and North of England on 6.5 per cent.[8]

This catastrophic employment decline caused the Wales TUC, unhappy about the rate at which new jobs were trickling through the pipeline, to take an initiative to explore alternatives to the inward investment policies of the Welsh Office, Welsh Development Agency and Development Board for Rural Wales. The Wales TUC was also of the opinion that the manner in which jobs lost had been bought-off by the payment of compensation to individual workers was unsatisfactory. A more productive use of redundancy payments would be to seek to generate new job opportunities, it was argued. The prospects for achieving this alternative use of compensation took on an air of practicality when it was realised that an estimated £58 million had been paid to redundant workers in Wales *in 1980 alone*. Of course, the financial risk to individuals investing in an untried venture meant that, realistically, there was little hope of tapping this fund for productive purposes unless and until some hard thinking and research were undertaken which might justify such risk-taking on the part of individual workers.

Research into Co-operative Potential

The Wales TUC, therefore, formulated a research proposal to investigate the broad potential of Worker Co-operatives as the means of generating some new employment in Wales. More specifically, the research was intended to assess the feasibility of achieving two objectives: first, the establishment of a Welsh Co-operative Resource Centre; and second, an independent Investment Fund for Wales. The research proposal was submitted to the Welsh Office in 1980 and £45,000 was advanced to assist the project by the Welsh Office and the Welsh Development Agency. The research involved obtaining detailed projections of future job losses and job needs on an industrial sector basis, then investigating, both theoretically and practically, the prospects for achieving substantial employment growth in the co-operative segment of the labour market.

This latter point was clearly of the first importance for three reasons. First, the scale of job loss in Wales demanded that attempts to generate new employment should be more than mere tokenism. Second, small businesses (including co-operatives) in Wales tend to be very small even though numerically there are more of them per 100,000 population than in the UK generally.[9] Despite this, small businesses have clearly made a negligible impact on overcoming Wales' unemployment problem. Finally, evidence on survival rates of co-operatives in countries other than Britain suggested that larger concerns were at no special disadvantage. In Britain, however, many factors, not the least being financial constraints built into the law governing co-operative practice, meant that few had been able to grow to the size of many of their foreign counterparts.

A renowned, successful example of a large industrial co-operative and one which was studied in depth in the research project was the Mondragon complex in the Basque country where 17,000 jobs exist in units of an average size of 300 employees. But elsewhere, for example in Italy, there are many examples of producer co-operatives employing hundreds of workers. Overall, 400,000 people are employed in co-operatives in Italy. Interestingly, some of the best established are those found in regions such as Emilia-Romagna where the Italian Communist Party has operated a co-operative development policy backed by substantial funding. In the food-producing industry (e.g. Parma ham, tomatoes, etc.) the middle-man has been virtually wiped out as co-operatives have developed the capacity to process output 'from field to food-shop'. The French, Spanish and American experiences of worker co-operatives were also explored. The general conclusion was that foreign experience implied that co-operative production was better integrated and developed than in Britain, and its positive aspects had been severely underestimated here.[10]

The experience of existing co-operatives in Wales was found to be comparable to that of such enterprise elsewhere in Britain. Closer attention to product marketing was seen to be essential if new ventures were to succeed. Also, the need for outside counselling, support and training was recognised, given the unevenness in response from local authorities and other official agencies in different parts of Wales. Another weakness was skills-imbalance. Most co-operatives lacked adequate managerial skills, especially in sales, marketing, financial and budgetary control. One effect of these imbalances is that the in-built tendency towards self-exploitation by co-operative workers becomes aggravated. But the financial constraints operating in the context of co-operative enterprise are even greater contributors to this self-exploitive condition. Lack of adequate finance leads to workers making sacrifices on wages to yield up what is appropriately known as "sweat equity".

The conclusions to the research undertaken were fourfold. First, it was clear that viable worker co-operatives could be established, but to be satisfactory alternatives to production for private, as against collective profit, financial involvement by members required substantial supplementation. Second, the local nature of the resources upon which co-operatives draw, and often the markets to which they relate, is a handicap. Low levels of locally generated capital limit the projected size to which co-operatives can develop. Alternative, non-local input and output linkages are needed. Thirdly, co-operatives, once established, unanimously reveal their main functional weakness to lie in *marketing*, a factor which requires the closest attention. And finally, external guidance and advice on other aspects of production, such as the development of business plans, managerial expertise and so on, would meet a widespread demand.

In other words, the Wales TUC found the case for establishing a resources centre and some form of external financing to be vitally necessary to the future health of the worker co-operative movement. On that basis the General Council accepted the recommendations of the research team that a resources centre should be established without delay and that the possibility of generating finance outside the normal channels should be pursued by the resource centre team.

Resourcing: the Wales Co-operative Development and Training Centre

As a result, the Wales TUC established the Wales Co-operative Development and Training Centre[11] in Cardiff in 1983, funded jointly 50:50 by the Welsh Office and the European Economic Community. The number of co-operatives to which this centre relates numbered approximately 30 in 1983. One of its first main efforts has been directed at co-ordinating the marketing and sales aspects of the co-operatives by linking them to the Co-operative Trades Fair held in Kensington and sponsored by the Greater London Enterprise Board, the West Midlands Enterprise Board, the Royal Arsenal Co-operative and the Co-operative Union. Over 100 co-operatives were represented there, 50 from London and 40 from the regions, of which 12 were from Wales. The Fair is one way of presenting to the public, to buyers, and other co-operatives the professional face of the co-operative movement.

The other main activity in which the resources centre has been involved is working on the problem of financing co-operative enterprise. The problem is that most government schemes ease financial obstacles to enterprises having share capital but co-operatives are not usually eligible because they do not issue shares. But recently the broader co-operative movement has been working out a system of Employee Participation Co-operatives. These could issue shares to employees but buy them back when they leave the co-operative. This could be the mechanism for releasing large sums of venture capital from the private market. Clearly, most banks and private venture capital agencies would remain unfriendly to even this alternative. So it is anticipated that the first approaches would be made to sources of 'friendly' capital — pension funds, enterprise board funds and EEC funds. The last-named is keen to support experimental methods of production, much more so than, for example, the British government with its obsession with numbers of jobs per pound spent.

Conclusions

Efforts are plainly at a very preliminary stage, but the Welsh approach of seeking to set up a framework within which worker co-operatives may flourish and, it is hoped, grow in output and employment terms is clearly based on a correct reading of the chequered history of co-operative enterprise in Britain. Given such a framework, which of course is nowhere near existence in Wales as yet, the possibilities for alternative methods of production as well as products will be that much greater. The signs are already there, in the Wales Co-operative Development and Training Centre, that priorities have been worked out, with the emphasis placed on marketing and finance. If the effort and enthusiasm which co-operatives usually engender in their workforces can be provided with a secure and professional basis, the collective rewards will be the greater.

Footnotes

1. H. Francis and D. Smith (1980), *The Fed, a History of the South Wales Miners in the Twentieth Century*, London, Lawrence and Wishart, p.15.
2. The Lucas Plan is summarised in Lucas Aerospace Shop Stewards' Committee (no date), *Lucas, An Alternative Plan*, Nottingham, Institute for Workers' Control, and extensively discussed in H. Wainwright and D. Elliott, *The Lucas Plan*, London, Allison and Busby. The Vickers Plan is outlined in, for example, Vickers National Combine Committee of Shop Stewards (no date), *Alternative Employment for Naval Shipbuilding Workers*, and *Building a Chieftain Tank and the Alternative*, Newcastle, Benwell Community Development Project. The background and content of the Vickers Plan is extensively discussed in H. Beynon and H. Wainwright (1979), *The Workers' Report on Vickers*, London, Pluto.
3. For a fuller account see R. Hudson and D. Sadler (forthcoming), Region, Class and the Politics of Steel Closures in the European Community, *Society and Space*.
4. An account of this effort is given in P. Cooke (1981), *Individual and Agency Responses to Mass Redundancy in the Steel Industry of Youngstown, Ohio*, London, Manpower Services Commission. The detailed report is published by National Centre for Economic Alternatives (1978), *Youngstown Demonstration Planning Project. Final Report*, Washington D.C., National Centre for Economic Alternatives.
5. Telechiric devices mimic in real time the actions of skilled workers, they do not absorb human knowledge, they respond to it. See M. Cooley and H. Wainwright (1981), The Lucas Plan: Its Lessons for Labour, *New Socialist*, 2, 13-16.
6. N. Hood and S. Young (1980), *European development strategies of US-owned manufacturing companies located in Scotland*, Edinburgh, HMSO.
7. The source of this estimate is the Wales TUC evidence to the Select Committee on Welsh Affairs as reported in Welsh Affairs Committee (1980), *The role of the Welsh Office and associated bodies in developing employment opportunities in Wales*, Vol.2, London, HMSO.
8. A. Townsend, (1982), *The Impact of Recession*, London, Croom Helm.
9. This fact undermines the conventional wisdom that Wales lacks small businesses because of some native lack of entrepreneurial skill. To the extent that entrepreneurs are lacking in some parts of Wales, such as the southern coalfield, this can be explained in terms of the low esteem in which such people have traditionally been held by miners and steelworkers and their families. This is interestingly discussed in C. Logan and D. Gregory (1981), *Co-operation and Job Creation in Wales: a Feasibility Study*, Cardiff, Wales TUC.
10. C. Logan and D. Gregory (1981), *ibid.*, pp.29-44.
11. I am grateful for information regarding the Wales Co-operative Development and Training Centre supplied by its manager, Mr Barry Cooper.

CHAPTER EIGHT

Production for Development — Alternatives from the Third World

Chris Lee

Newly independent countries, dazzled by the manufacturing achievements in Europe of their former colonial masters, set out on courses of development which followed the 'modern, Western model'. Investment in capital-intensive, high-technology industrialisation built vast hydroelectric dams, equipped modern factories and produced consumer goods for the rich urban elites, while the rural masses went hungry. Third World government planners, trained in Western ways and housed in showcase administrative buildings, invested heavily in urban and industrial growth leaving little capital to help small-scale manufacturers, small farmers and landless labourers.

In agriculture, investment was concentrated on production of cash crops for export while cereal production for local consumption stagnated. In the mid-1930s Africa was a cereal exporter, by 1950 the continent was self-sufficient but by 1976 it had to import 10 million tonnes and just two years later, the figure was 12 million tonnes.[1]

In Central America, for over a century, cash crop production has dominated agricultural development with large plantations growing coffee and bananas for export to markets all over the world. In the last few decades government investors, backed by international financial institutions such as the World Bank and the Inter-American Development Bank, have biased their support in favour of cash crop production. In Guatemala the government set up the National Agrarian Bank for financing of agriculture. From 1964 to 1973, 87 per cent of the bank's agricultural credit went to finance crops grown for export while only 3 per cent went to small farmers growing staple food crops such as rice, corn and beans.[2]

Multinational Investment

As large-scale food production has grown in Central America, foreign multinational companies have been quick to exploit and control the changes. A range of North American multinational giants have joined the long established banana companies such as United Fruit in the region. Two-thirds of all United States agribusiness subsidiaries in the Third World are now located in Latin America.[3] Their operations in Central America have diversified from direct landowning into supplying the region's growing market for agricultural inputs — fertilizers, pesticides and tractors.

Nor do employment prospects from this agribusiness give cause for hope. For the majority of plantation workers — peasants forced off their land or unable to survive by farming — their new-found work is a doubtful improvement. Del Monte's 4,500 workers in Guatemala, for example, live on the plantation itself, isolated from the local town, in housing which is at best spartan. Wages are far from adequate for proper food and clothing, hours of work are long and conditions are tough.[4]

In Africa, the story is much the same. European household names such as Brooke Bond, Nestle and Unilever dominate trade in traditional crops of coffee, tea, cocoa, palm oil and rubber and are now expanding into flower, fruit and vegetable production. They wield enormous power in the production process with their own plantations, processing plants, agricultural input supply (Shell and ICI produce fertilizers and seeds) and control over sales, marketing and distribution. These companies shape Africa's agricultural output to feed their own profits but not the majority of African mouths.[5] (In 1973, International Labour Office figures suggested that two-thirds of the people in Africa were living in conditions of extreme poverty with 10 million people being unemployed and 53 million markedly under-employed, most of them in villages.[6])

Land and Power

Such is the scale of the problem for the rural poor in the Third World that there is a great temptation to suggest that access to *any* employment which allows those people to go some way towards meeting their basic needs — for food, clothing, housing, education and basic health care — must be a step in the right direction. This argument, however, espoused by multinational plantation owners to justify their exploitative employment practices, is one which fails to acknowledge that if jobs are to bring lasting improvements they must give workers not only payment but power.

The Indian tea pickers, the Guatemalan plantation workers, the bonded labourers — they are landless, powerless and poor.

Even for small landowning farmers, their futures are held in the hands of others when access to irrigation, credit facilities and extension services may be dependent on having political clout in higher places. Nor does productivity guarantee an income when prices are determined by 'market forces' beyond the control of the small producer. In countries where land ownership is concentrated in the hands of a few, as is the case throughout most of the Third World, who benefits from agricultural production depends on who owns the land and who has the machinery to work it. The promise of the 'Green Revolution' — increased crop yields for all — was empty for all but a few. Those with the capital to risk on new hybrid crops invested in high-cost inputs of fertilizers, weedkillers and pesticides and so increased productivity. The net result is that the rich get richer and, as imported capital-intensive, energy-hungry mechanisation takes over, the poor and the powerless get hungrier.

Alternatives to poverty?

Multinational investors in agribusiness all over the world wield enormous power and influence over Third World governments' agricultural policies for cash crop production in preference to production of food crops for local consumption. Local rural development initiatives which try to bring change from the bottom up may stand a better chance of success than those which try to beat the multinationals at their own game. Small-scale projects to create productive employment and generate income may also have a better chance of bringing lasting improvements to the conditions of the poorest groups in the rural sector. Projects which give power to the producers — control over marketing, distribution and pricing through collective organisation — may in turn help to influence government policies at least at local levels.

Foreign-aided Rural Development — Two Case Studies

The means by which workers gain power are a constant concern for foreign aid agencies with input into rural development projects, particularly when such involvement includes provision of volunteer personnel. Even in a training role, the very presence of (usually) white, Western 'expertise' can easily create a dependent relationship, a sense of powerlessness among local people. Enlightened volunteer-sending agencies, learning from past experience, are trying to translate this knowledge into projects which enable people to learn to take charge of their own lives and to solve their own problems. Such

its members for collective organisation of production and marketing. Furthermore, Botswana's tradition of 'village consultation' (by which village chiefs make decisions in discussions with the local people) may provide the seedbed for creation of a democratic organisation. A prerequisite for any such development however, must surely be the introduction of a comprehensive programme in co-operative education.

Co-operative Juan XXIII, Panama [8]

Juan XXIII is a multi-service co-operative centred on a town of 35,000, Santiago, in the province of Veraguas about four miles by road from Panama City. It serves an area of about 40 miles radius in a country two-thirds the size of England with a population of just two million.

Panama is a country of great inequality: enormous wealth in Panama City (a centre for international finance with strong United States economic and military influence along the canal zone) but great poverty in hilly rural parts of the country. Farming is difficult with acid soils, undulating terrain and a wet season for eight months of the year. Farm sizes vary enormously. The biggest ranches in the plains are owned by millionaires who breed cattle for export while smaller wealthy farmers in the hilly areas grow coffee, also for export, and breed dairy cattle to supply the Panamanian milk market. In the province of Veraguas in the mid-1960s, subsistence farmers were predominant and villages had no electricity, water supply or sanitation.

About 220 mainly small farmers came together in 1966 to set up the co-operative Juan XXIII. They were supported by a group of priests who at that time were engaged in a literacy and 'awareness creation' programme designed to show the poor the causes of their poverty and ways of overcoming them. Identifying a lack of government support for small producers and their inability to control market prices for their produce, Juan XXIII was set up with funding from an overseas church agency. A small shop was opened selling basic agricultural equipment, including hammers, spades and machetes. A tractor was also purchased with the initial grant but soon proved to be a big mistake since not only was maintenance costly and petrol expensive but people didn't really know how to use it.

Today, having struggled through difficult times and near collapse, Juan XXIII has 1,400/1,500 members, sells about US$5 million worth of produce, employs 120/130 people and has assets of about US$1 million. Retailing activities are the main sources of profit for re-investing — community shops in the villages and supermarkets in the town sell mainly imported produce and some produced by members. The co-operative also has other functions. A rotating loan scheme which enables members to purchase inputs such as seed and fertilizer. Marketing — buying produce from farmers for sale in the community shops (where local village committees have influence over retail prices) or in the city. Production — a processing plant supplies feedstuffs to co-op members and three trained agronomists offer free advice.

The creation of the co-operative was the first popular step in Panama to confront the problems facing the rural poor. Conditions have changed a lot in Veraguas since 1966 — many of the less isolated communities now have electricity, running water and proper sanitation. Juan XXIII has helped the local people to force along and take advantage of the economic development of the area. In developing this participatory self-help role for its members, the co-operative's highly democratic decision making structure has been of fundamental importance.

The power of Juan XXIII as a popular organisation is reflected in its changing relations with the national government. The government had no part in its creation but, as it and other co-ops in Panama grew, a 'ministry of co-ops' was set up and, through the Agricultural Development Bank, channelled loans (about a third of current financing) to the co-operative and its members. The government tries to monitor and control the organisation through its powers of auditing and through regional advisers but the power of the co-operative in relation to the government derives from two sources. Firstly, in the province of Veraguas where trade unions offer little opposition to the 'establishment', Juan XXIII is the biggest popular organisation with means of mass protest. Secondly, as a successful co-operative, unlike most others in the province, it repays its loans and is therefore in a stronger bargaining position.

Co-operative Juan XXIII is now entirely run by local people. In its 17 year history, two events may be singled out as important for motivation, instilling as they did a determination in the members of the co-operative without which the whole organisation might have collapsed. The first event was associated with the purchase of the tractor in the early days. Its rapid demise to the status of a white elephant, wasting much of the initial church agency grant, raised doubts in the minds of the supporting priests about the future of the co-operative. Near bankruptcy followed but almost as if to prove the priests wrong and to silence the cynics in the town (which traditionally looks down on the rural sector) the co-op members struggled on, independent of church support. Another adversity that probably

CHAPTER NINE

Arms Conversion and the Labour Movement

David Pelly

The conversion of military production facilities to civilian uses — 'arms conversion' — has become a central issue for the labour movement in recent years because of a confluence of developments at a political and economic level. Public support for nuclear disarmament has continued to grow; the burgeoning defence budget is becoming an ever-increasing burden on a weak economy; the Labour Party is now committed to unilateral disarmament and to limiting defence spending, and this Government is pressing ahead with cuts in defence staff, base closures and the privatisation of certain services and installations like the Royal Ordnance Factories (ROF's).

There is a growing disjuncture between the costs of defence spending in terms of lost jobs or the threat of thermonuclear war, and the benefits which are alleged to be derived from it, in terms of 'security', export orders or technological spin-offs.

The challenge facing the labour and peace movements is to come up with clear proposals for redirecting resources from the military to the civilian sectors without causing economic dislocation and loss of employment. This is the central element of an arms conversion programme. The task is by no means an easy one, however, because the pace of the developments already described require an immediate response. It is not possible to draw up a series of plans for arms conversion and then await the election of a sympathetic government and the implementation of the plans. A strategy is required which will link the pressing problems of base closures, for example, with the development of a new approach to foreign policy and the role of the Armed Forces.

Such a strategy would not simply be of relevance in the area of defence policy but would also demonstrate in a realistic way how the economy could be planned and oriented towards production for need, rather than for profit. Yet, if arms conversion is going to make any progress a number of critical issues have to be confronted head-on, rather than side-stepped which is what has tended to occur.

Defence Policy

The extent of an arms conversion programme is determined by the discrepancy between the level of existing military production capacity and that required to fulfil future defence programmes or meet budget requirements. Thus, a programme of arms conversion should reflect changes in the requirement for military systems and equipment, as determined by defence policy. Arms conversion is only therefore a means to an end rather than an objective in itself. At present arms conversion has either been supported *in principle* by the Labour Party and a number of trade unions at a national level, or it has taken the form of localised plans which have been put forward by groups of workers in military industries — aerospace or shipbuilding — in response to particular problems, such as the loss of major defence contracts. No attempt has been made to make any concrete connection between the two. This is largely a consequence of the labour movement's failure to develop a coherent alternative to the established defence policy.

Without any clear policies regarding the need for a deep-water Navy, long range strike aircraft, a strong presence on the Rhine or a major commitment to NATO it is difficult to predict what military equipment requirements will be and, in consequence, what military production facilities will be surplus and need 'converting' to alternative uses.

The lack of clarity on this issue was made obvious during the 1983 Election. The Labour Party not only failed to exploit the contradictions of the Conservative Party's policies by highlighting, for example, the economic costs of the high defence budget. It also failed to make any effective response to the unsubstantiated allegation that Labour's proposals would lead to the loss of 300,000 jobs. Instead of confronting the logical consequences of nuclear disarmament and limits on defence spending, which without countermeasures would lead to job loss, and proposing appropriate action in the form of detailed conversion plans, the Labour representatives tried to argue that they were not making significant cuts in defence spending. They were committed to "reducing defence expenditure to the average proportion of the gross domestic product (GDP) spent by other European countries in NATO", but by assuming that Britain's GDP would be higher under Labour they managed to suggest that the level of defence expenditure would not be

important issue from the mid-70s and not at the height of the 'Ban The Bomb' movement in the 1950s is a consequence of the juxtaposition of two issues — disarmament and employment.

The power of the Plan was its ability to mobilise support by presenting proposals that were a practical, concrete and apparently achievable alternative to the immediate problems facing the workforce. Yet it was also extremely audacious in conventional industrial relations terms both in its rejection of existing Corporate policy and its challenge to managerial prerogative over a range of decisions regarding product choice, capital investment, the organisation of the production process and so on.

The fact that the Plan was so far reaching in scope probably contributed to its rejection, as a complete proposal, by management. It was, of course, fundamentally a trade union initiative which extended collective bargaining into new areas. It was *not* simply a series of product suggestions. The Plan caught the imagination of other trade unionists because it overcame some of the shortcomings of purely defensive struggles against redundancy and it enabled those working in the defence sector to reconcile their campaigns against redundancy with their commitment to reductions in defence spending. Alternative plans were also instigated in other defence contractors like Vickers and the British Aircraft Corporation (BAC) and outside of the defence sector in the power engineering industry, Dunlop and other companies.

The Lucas Plan created waves of interest which spread across Europe stimulating a number of Conversion initiatives. In West Germany, a number of Alternative Product Working Groups (Arbeitskreise Alternative Fertigung) have been set up in several of the major military contractors, including Blohm & Voss, AEG, MBB, Krupp and MAK. Most of the conversion activity has involved the German Metalworkers Trade Union, IG Metall, which is the main organiser in the defence sector. These working groups were established to examine problems of job insecurity, mainly arising from the termination or loss of contracts (both civilian and military) and some of the groups have elaborated a number of alternative product proposals. These have varied from the ambitious Combined Heat and Power Systems in Blohm and Voss, to more modest proposals for tyre re-cycling equipment in Voith in Bremen. Nevertheless, while progress has been made in drawing up product proposals no prototypes have yet been built as the groups have not been able to 'liberate' resources from their employers or utilise the facilities of units like CAITS, which was established by the

Lucas Combine to develop aspects of their Plan. However, the position is now changing as a number of Innovation and Technical Advice Centres are set up in cities like Osnabruck and Bremen. These centres are sponsored by unions, universities and local authorities and are concerned with a number of problems at work — new technology, product development, health and safety etc.

The Working Groups face a similar degree of opposition from management that the Lucas Combine encountered in Britain. In that sense, the lack of prototypes is less of a problem than the lack of power to force management to develop or produce them. At present the Working Groups are not part of the Works Councils (Betriebsrat) which exercise considerable influence over industrial relations in the factories in Germany, and so the question of Alternative Products or Conversion has rarely been raised in the established negotiating or consultative structures. This has made it difficult to make 'alternative products' central to campaigns against redundancies.

In AEG, for example, Working Groups were set up in a number of factories in response to the publication of management plans for closures and mass redundancies. AEG was heavily involved in manufacturing marine, power engineering and telecommunication systems. Over 70 per cent of the latter was for military application. The main proposals to come out of the Working Groups were a new local transport system for Berlin based on the renovation of the high-speed railway (S-Bahn) and a 'block-heat energy' power station for Berlin's district heating system. The proposals would have provided work both in AEG and some other companies like Siemens through the manufacture of power supply, telecommunication and related equipment. But as these plans were being put forward AEG committed itself 'irrevocably' to its planned closures. Since management refused to consider the alternative production proposals, the implementation of these plans became dependent upon obtaining state support for the establishment of independent enterprises run by the workforce. This support was not forthcoming.

Although more progress has been made with Conversion proposals in other companies like Blohm and Voss, none of them have been taken up for production by management. This is a fairly accurate reflection of the progress of Conversion proposals in other countries like Italy or Sweden or Belgium. Even the Lucas Plan, which is probably the most comprehensive example of a trade union conversion plan, now seems unlikely to be fulfilled as the Combine have reached an impasse with

two versions would be examined in a bargaining context though, in the case of disagreement, a specially appointed Minister could intervene as arbitrator. These conversion proposals clearly recognise the conflictual element of industrial planning and therefore give greater consideration to support for trade union plans.

Yet although these discussions about national conversion planning are important and deal with fundamental issues relating to the intervention of a Labour government in industry, to many people the debate is almost academic because it does not really address itself to the current problems of workers in the defence sector. This is the second criticism of the current Labour Party Conversion proposals — that they are predicated on the election of a Labour government which is unlikely to happen for some time yet.

The prospects of an arms conversion initiative like the Lucas Plan being implemented now are much worse than they were eight years ago when the Lucas Plan was first proposed. There are three main reasons for this:

1. The effect of the recession has been to depress the market for a whole number of civilian goods making it difficult within the context of the 'free' market to identify new, alternative products which could form the basis for conversion or even diversification.
2. As non-military public expenditure is cut back and nationalised industries and services are privatised, the possibility of using the public sector as the market for alternative products is smaller. In fact the labour movement is finding it difficult to defend the public sector as it stands, let alone extend its influence.
3. High levels of unemployment combined with a joint offensive on organised labour by the state and the employers has shifted the balance of power firmly back in capital's favour, thereby reducing the capacity of trade unions to force changes on management.

Arms Conversion in the Future

The next couple of years will clearly be a testing time both for campaigns for nuclear disarmament and arms conversion. To date arms conversion has performed two roles. One has been ideological, demonstrating that people and resources could be employed in the manufacture of peaceful goods and not weapons of mass destruction. The other has been practical, presenting a new approach to trade union struggles against closures. Where arms conversion has been most successful in mobilising people it has been where these two roles were combined, as with Lucas in the mid-1970s.

Unfortunately, the political milieu of the 1980s is different for the three reasons already described. This has totally undermined the second of arms conversion's two roles — as a strategy for securing employment. Management have completely ignored conversion proposals unless they have identified particular product proposals which appear viable according to conventional market criteria. Major redundancies have occurred in Lucas, Vickers, British Aerospace, AEG, MBB, McDonnell Douglas, Lockheed and many other military contractors, despite the existence of coherent trade union plans for securing employment through conversion in several of these companies.

This presents a large difficulty for the proponents of arms conversion since for many workers in the defence sector it no longer represents an achievable alternative to redundancies. Thus, arms conversion has tended to take on a simply ideological function which is valuable as a weapon in fighting the crude monetarism and militarism of this Government but not sufficient to win support at shop-floor level. In fact there is a danger that arms conversion proposals may become mere rhetoric, with no industrial base.

So, the position of defence workers is becoming increasingly critical. Job insecurity and pressure for nuclear disarmament necessitate the development of concrete conversion proposals but external forces severely limit the chances of their success. Conversely, attempts to create the right political framework for conversion have little immediate relevance to defence workers. The present challenge is to draw the short and longer term elements of arms conversion together.

The first 'point of departure' has to be the development of a coherent defence policy, as was argued earlier. Clear priorities have to be laid out and then worked through to assess the implications for procurement and employment. For example, if the Government renounced nuclear weapons but decided to replace them with modern conventional weapons, leaving its defence policies more or less unchanged, then this could result in a considerable *increase* in defence spending. This would be a defeat for one of the major economic arguments for disarmament. At the same time the clarification of defence policy will make it easier to distinguish between the employment problems of workers in the Nuclear Weapons Research Establishment at Aldermaston and those in the ROF's. Different plans would then follow in each case.

This process will remove a lot of the confusion that exists

FROM ARMS TO . .

WE NEED TO BRING THE IDEA OF 'FROM SWORDS TO PLOUGHSHARES' INTO THE LATE C20th AS AN EVERYDAY VISION.

FFICE WORK

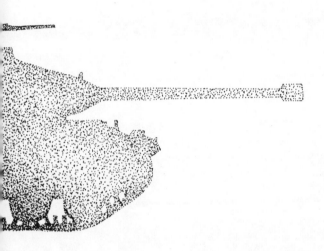

WE NEED TO BE ABLE TO ARGUE FROM TANKS TO TRACTORS, FROM MISSILES TO MENTAL WELL BEING.
WE NEED . . .

CHAPTER TEN

Arms Conversion: A View from the USA

Seymour Melman

In the nations of Western capitalism, especially in England and the United States, there are two classes of problems whose solution requires conversion of major industrial and other resources to socially useful work. The first problem stems from the drain on production resources owing to the operation of a long-enduring military economy. The second set of problems stems from the concentration of managers in civilian economy on profit-making even without production.

The role of military economy in detracting from the production of socially useful products is ordinarily masked by the acceptance of price as a common denominator of economic product. From this vantage point, accepted by virtually all economists, an economic good is denoted by the presence of price, independently of the presence of ordinary economic use values: usefulness for consumption or usefulness for further production.

The Military Capital Fund and Civilian Capital Formation

From the standpoint of an economics of production, the meaning of a modern military budget is properly understood to be a capital fund. The physical resources that are set in motion by a military budget correspond to what is ordinarily termed, within the industrial enterprise, fixed capital and working capital. The magnitude of capital resources used for the military is best understood when these are related to the scale of civilian capital formation. From the ordinary categories in the national income accounts we can derive a useful estimate of new civilian fixed capital formation ('gross domestic fixed capital formation') to which we can compare the military capital fund. From the data for 1979 (last year of data compiled by the UN) we know that for every $100 of new civilian capital formation in the United States $33 were expended for the military. In England this relationship was $32 to the military for every $100 for fresh civilian capital. It is significant that in Germany this relationship was $20 to each $100 and in Japan $3.7 to each $100. The manifestly smaller quantity of capital resources devoted by the German and Japanese economies to the military enterprise goes far to account for the modernity of their factories and the high quality of the infrastructure features of those societies.

The Decay of Civilian Industry

The contrast with the condition of British and American industry is dramatic. In these countries the decay of civilian industry and infrastructure stands in sharp contrast to the technological innovation and sophistication of the military enterprise.

The prospects here are grim indeed. For the United States we can estimate that by 1988 the ratio of military to civilian use of capital will climb to 87:100 owing to the present military expansion plans of the American government. This promises to speed industrial and infrastructure decay in the United States. Indeed, it is entirely possible that a set of conditions can be reached constituting a 'point of no return' so that it will be difficult or unfeasible to set in motion any major process of industrial and infrastructure reconstruction. The point then is plain: the $2,089 billions planned for the military enterprise from 1981 to 1988 take away from the civilian enterprise. Those resources must be transferred to civilian account if an economic renewal is ever to be carried out.

Changes in Industrial Management

The second major source of industrial decay in the United States and England is the transformation of industrial management. At one time, industrial managers characteristically had both an interest in and a competence for the organisation of work. It was ordinarily understood that competence in the organisation of production was the preferred path to managerial fame and fortune. The decades following World War II included a major alteration in management institutions. Profits could be earned without the burdens of production organisation and the requirement to cope with the myriad problems of industrial operations. Strategic financial moves have been given the first place in the agenda of strategies for which modern managements are trained and equipped. Profit-making is carried out by extra-production methods. Indeed, swift financial manoeuvres are often facilitated by the absence of responsibility

economic conversion planning also has a major political effect: the society is thereby better prepared, and therefore more competent, to enter into negotiations for halting and reversing an international arms race.

Renewal of Manufacturing Industry

The second major type of industrial planning pertains to the industrial renewal of manufacturing and other facilities that have been allowed to go into disrepair owing to the short-term, profit-maximising and production-minimising character of finance-oriented managers. For these industries the issue is not what to produce, but how to produce competently. In the United States there is no shortage of demand for steel, automobiles, electron microscopes, household sewing machines, men's shoes, and many articles of clothing. There is a problem in those industries but it pertains to the inability of many of the US-based firms and factories to produce quality products at a competitive price. The scale of this disability is often not appreciated. Therefore, I include here a table of data from *Profits Without Production* to show the proportion of the market for given classes of goods within the United States that is now served from factories located outside the US. Each of the percentages shown here also refers to the same proportion of the former labour force of that industry which is now without opportunity for productive livelihood.

Percentage of US Consumption Produced Abroad (1979-80)

Product	%	Product	%
Automobiles	27	Integrated microcircuits	34
Machine tools	25*	X-ray and other irradiation equipment	24
Steel mill products	15		
TV sets, black and white	87	Motion-picture cameras (1977)	74
Calculating machines, hand-held	47	Sewing machines (1978)	51
desk-top and printing	39	Tape recorders and dictating machines, office type	100
Microwave ranges and ovens	22	Bicycles	22
Communications systems and equipment	16	Apparel	20
		Leather gloves	37
		Footwear (non-rubber)	45
		Flatware	50

*As of 1982, this figure is 42 per cent.

It is crucial to understand that there is nothing indigenous to the United States that prevents competent performance in these industries. Indeed, it is characteristic of a great array of manufacturing industries that when their component factories are ranked by measures of output per man-hour then the top quarter of firms shows an average productivity per person employed more than two times the productivity of the lowest quarter of firms. This means that it has been possible to meet American costs, including American wages, with appropriate mechanisation and organisation of work. But finance-oriented managers who are eager to maximise short-term profits have not been interested in making investments necessary for modernising plant and equipment.

In this array of industries, and the others taking on these depleted characteristics, the problem is essentially one of increasing decision-making power in the hands of the producing occupations. They alone have both an interest in, and a competence for, the conduct of production work in a manner to be technically and economically competent.

Both national and other planning for economic renewal in countries that have suffered grave depletion of industrial competence requires a separate identification of the problems of conversion from military to civilian economy, and the problems of industrial renewal which calls for diminishing the controls of profit-maximising and production-minimising decision makers.

production has seriously been mooted are arms manufacturers. This means that they sell primarily to one unique customer — the government. This is an environment quite different from that governing the behaviour of most businesses. They have to produce what 'the market' will buy, and in this case the market is an abstract faceless thing. If they can't produce goods that compete with what other firms are making they will not survive.

By comparison, the degree of flexibility which arms firms potentially enjoy is enormous. After all, arms are really little more than a modern version of pyramids or cathedrals — they don't actually do anything. If arms production stopped tomorrow it wouldn't really matter, except, of course, in the export sectors of the industry. In this respect, the scope for alternative production is infinitely greater in these industries.

This means that we need to look at other industries differently. Only a tenth of the manufacturing workforce are directly employed on defence, with not quite as many again employed indirectly. Only three industries — shipbuilding, aerospace, and parts of electronics — are heavily involved with arms. These are concentrated only in particular parts of Britain, with very few major branches in Wales for example.

Third, different kinds of companies and different parts of the same company, have very different technical processes. One of the major decisions large firms spend a lot of time thinking about is how to distribute the work to their constituent parts to get the best use of labour and to retain the maximum degree of control. Since the 1960s British industry has undergone a widespread transformation, energetically splitting off the various different bits of work and allocating them selectively to different branches, in many cases shifting work to distant parts of the country and transforming it with new machinery. The end result is a complex network. Some parts of the country get the branch factories, while others get the central office which operates as the brain of the system. The typical branch factory is given very specific duties and machinery and staff are specialised accordingly. It is therefore very inflexible, for both technical and social reasons. In the motor industry, for example, the technicians, advanced computer programmers, and key design engineers are mostly located in the Midlands. Branch factories in Wales get stuck with the routine work. The central unit has the technical potential to turn itself to a variety of tasks, but the branch unit cannot easily change without being ripped apart and rebuilt.

This flexibility isn't solely a matter of the machinery which is installed. It is equally a matter of the kind of experience and training which the workforce gets. The central departments specialise in keeping an eye on the market and on competitors, and on technical developments in the field. Being knowledgeable and living in an 'information rich' environment is what they are there for. The opposite is the case in the branch factory. It isn't supposed to know what is going on, or why it does what it does.

It is possible to sketch roughly those parts of Britain where the 'rich' work environment may be found. This is an environment which offers a good job, and one that few people will be allowed the chance to experience. Being the best jobs, they tend also to be located in what company managers think are the best places. It appears that what this group of white, male, middle-class and middle aged decision makers likes is the green and pleasant land of middle England with access to Heathrow. They key departments in modern industry, especially electronics, but also many office-based industries such as insurance, tend to lie in an area (sometimes called the 'Sunbelt' US fashion) roughly between Cambridge, Portsmouth and Bristol. The main exceptions are to be found in the old heavy industries — many of them arms industries — which are still tied to dockyards or other sites in the North, but their days are numbered.

The limited information environment imposed in most workplaces extends to information about other workers. In most rural areas and a good many cities, too, workers are not able to learn what their brother and sister workers are doing, even in the same company. The 'coverage' of trades unions is extremely thin — and getting thinner — so they rarely provide a channel for creating the kind of impressive nation-wide linkage that Lucas Shop Stewards built. Indeed one of the reasons for setting up Branch plants outside the old industrial conurbations is precisely to exploit a fragmented workforce.

For all these reasons — market environment, industrial process, labour process — it is unrealistic to expect a widespread movement towards alternative production in the mould of the heroic examples of Lucas and the arms companies.

On the Periphery: A Thousand Flowers — Trying to Bloom

While the Lucas initiative was being developed, refined, and fought for, hundreds of smaller local initiatives, in all parts of the country, were also struggling to gain a foothold. Throughout the 1970s local groups from inner London to the Western Isles of Scotland began to experiment with new ways of creating jobs. In many of them the goals of socially useful products and of democratic working relations were important in engaging the sympathy and enthusiasm of a wide variety of people. Local employment initiatives, in places where a Lucas-type initiative is unimaginable, have become increasingly important as the recession has deepened — partly because they naturally tend to crop up in the places with the most acute need. For that reason the state has become interested in them: it has been estimated that over the European Community as a whole, over a million jobs have now been created in this way. It may be instructive to look at a few examples of these modest — and often inspiring — endeavours.

Llanaelhaearn is a small village in the Lleyn peninsula of North Wales. Like many such villages it has been gradually eroded by alternating tides of migration, bringing tourists and second-home purchasers in and taking young working people out. In the early 1960s a group of people in the village decided that the only effective way to do anything about this would be to create employment in Llanaelhaearn which would be under the control of the villagers themselves. The campaign — which built on a sense of local identity reinforced by the fact that nearly everyone spoke Welsh — was extraordinarily successful. Eventually a building was constructed and a private manufacturer from Birmingham moved in to make key rings. Six months later he departed. Confirmed in their view that they could no longer depend on cowboys from England, the villagers cast around for something to make that could provide jobs with reasonable security. They had the building and the labour. All that was needed was an alternative product. Eventually they stumbled across the idea of Celtic design knitwear, and they have been making it ever since.

However, this is not really a story with a happy ending. Employment in the factory became significant during the period when it was subsidised under the Job Creation Programme and the MSC's Training Workshop scheme. Since then it has dwindled to a couple of people. The real bottom line problem — far more intractable than anything else — was that the market had no room for what they could produce. Well-made pullovers cost more than many people care to pay. Only if the enterprise had expanded gigantically and installed mass production equipment could it have cut costs sufficiently to compete. But then the product would not have been 'different'.

At around the same time in South Wales a long-established toy factory closed down. Triang had kept it open for a few more years than they had intended only because the government handed them £4 million to do so. When this ran out they pulled out. Three hundred and fifty jobs were lost with the closure, and a campaign was launched to create an alternative source of work

for those who wanted to stay together. A co-operative was set
up, and ideas for what to make were canvassed. In 1979 a
sympathetic industrial and design consultant, who was involved
with co-ops elsewhere in South Wales, offered a plan for a
radical alternative use of their skills. The idea was to build a
small number of specialised 4-wheel drive cars, assembled from
parts which could be bought-in from existing British firms. If
they started with 100 people, he estimated, they could expect to
grow rapidly and re-employ all those who had worked at Triang,
and at least as many again.

However, this product never saw the light of day. The action
committee felt grave doubts about putting all their eggs in such
a risky basket. They were also more than a little suspicious of
the alternative design wizard who was behind this idea. So they
turned their attentions to humbler things. One of these was a
'Hobcart' for disabled children, an idea inspired by the Lucas
Plan. Eventually, however, very little came of this either. The
development of the prototype took so long that many co-op
members lost interest, and market openings proved to be few
and far between. One of the problems was that equipment was
already on the market from reputable private firms. It was
asking too much to expect a health authority already hard
pressed by cuts to set aside time and money for a shaky little
enterprise with no track record and an unfamiliar work style.

A final example from Wales: the Wales TUC has been trying
to set up a co-operative support agency modelled very loosely on
the system at Mondragon in the Basque country. Since it is
anxious to get viable companies established and to establish its
respectability in business circles, it has played down any
emphasis on alternative products. For all its impressive
ambitions, it too is forced to play within the rules set by the
market.

The fact that all these examples are from Wales shouldn't be
taken to imply there is something odd about the Welsh. Many
more equally sorry tales could be told about ventures in
England, from Lewisham to Taunton to Newcastle.

The Problem of Markets

The argument so far has suggested that the spaces for
experimentation in producing different things or producing
things in different ways is extremely limited. The kind of
enterprise that we can realistically expect to provide that space

invariably starts off with a whole heap of disadvantages.

The disadvantages in question are often thought to lie in the realm of traditional business problems — lack of start-up finance, lack of entrepreneurial wizardry, imbalance between production and marketing, etc., etc. A lot of co-operative enthusiasts talk as if these are the central issues. Certainly Wales TUC drew this lesson from its examination of the remarkable co-operative network in Mondragon, in the Basque country of Northern Spain. They argue that what is needed is special access to finance, special training facilities, and a special agency designed to dream up and develop product ideas which can then be taken on by co-operatives.

It is undoubtedly true that co-operatives and other experimental enterprise forms do suffer many disadvantages of the kind that is stressed in this sort of argument. They generally have only a fraction of the initial capital that private small businesses have, and by their very nature they are often less equipped with business expertise. But even if a friendly government (let's imagine) did provide generous help as some European countries have done, what would this achieve? It would assist the birth of a lot more small enterprises which were organised internally in a non-conventional way, but externally they would still be more or less like any other enterprise. This means they would have to fight their way through the controlled chaos of the market.

The market is, above all, the creature of the society of which it is a part. In an unequal, class-divided society, in which divisions between the sexes, the races, and even age groups, are maintained, different groups of people bring to the market different amounts of income. The demand patterns which result reflect the underlying inequalities. The market is a distributional mechanism which reflects the fact that some have much more power than others. In its turn, the market tends to keep things that way.

Socialist theory and practice has explored two ways of subordinating the market. Either it can be by-passed, by public sector production of goods aimed directly at meeting needs, or it can be shifted on its axis, by redistributing income to people who haven't got much. The first route is that of planning, and the second is that of redistribution. Each is hazardous in its own way. The planning route creates the problem of bureaucracy, as an elite of controllers decide what people 'really want'. Equally, the path of redistribution faces the enormous complications which arise when you try to interfere with the market a little bit at a time.

Socially Useful Production and the Local Economy

When people talk about the economy, especially on the Left, most attention is given to the international dimension, and multinational corporations are often identified as the heart of the system. This is certainly a vitally important aspect, but it is far from being the whole picture. In fact, what goes on in a particular town often bears only an oblique relation to it. Many vital services, a large number of manufacturing activities, and the bulk of employment are much more bound up with the local economy and the way in which it responds to the international segments. Most 'collective consumption goods' are produced and consumed locally — such things as education, welfare, amenities, many of which lie in the public sector. But a substantial proportion of private sector business is governed by the local economy, too, — notably construction, retailing, repairing and an enormous variety of personal services (pubs, clubs, restaurants, etc). To a large extent this local economic cluster is 'income dependent' in that the employment levels and incomes generated in it are governed by the stimulus coming from the non-local activities. To take an obvious example, the hotels, bars and small shops of Covent Garden depend on the spending of people who work in the City on internationally oriented activities, or on tourists.

To date, most local authorities have only intervened in their local economies in the mildest ways. Through a combination of central government constraints, and lack of sympathy or imagination, they have confined themselves to serving existing or conventional firms, with the occasional heavily publicised support to co-ops or small business initiatives. What they have never done is to take responsibility for the development of the local economy — neither attending to the supply side by creating new enterprises, nor fuelling the demand side by redistributing incomes (although many local activities, such as bus fare subsidies, do have an impact on this). Yet the impact of a conscious attempt to remould the links within the local economy and to structure the inter-action between the non-local economy and the local system could be enormous. It could certainly be enough to create a space for new activities which would both be desirable in themselves, and could provide models around which subsequent protests could mobilise.

It is fairly easy to think of some examples. In many rural areas, and also in those urban council estates which were dumped on the fringes of most cities in the 1930s and 1950s, it is often extremely difficult for people to get around unless they have a car. It is also frightening, especially for children, old people, and many women. Cheap accessible transport would meet a massive hidden need. This does not necessarily mean the provision of buses or railways. A municipal or subsidised taxi service would provide new jobs, while providing a socially useful product. The repair and maintenance of the vehicles would create a further demand for labour. Provided this was channelled appropriately it could give openings for non-traditional work styles and could be used to target jobs onto women and discriminated minorities without at the same time withdrawing jobs and income from workers elsewhere. The key to the whole process linking alternative production, employment, and a *de facto* redistribution of income to the poor, would be the initial subsidy.

Other needs such as cheap heating and better housing have been well documented elsewhere. There is hardly any disagreement that massive savings in energy consumption could easily be achieved by better insulation, while even in wettest Wales solar energy could cut heating costs dramatically. Moreover, the technology involved is simple and could easily be assembled on a local basis, again providing jobs.

Of course, the prerequisite for any experiments along these lines is — we are back with it — the need for more public spending. But this should be distinguished from the traditional Left demand which focuses on the amount and on the overall balance between private and public sector. In the perspective set-out here what matters is that the spending should lead to a remoulding of the local economy. Whether this takes place through municipal public agencies or via private firms is secondary. It is not a case of public sector good, private sector bad, but of subordinating the local needs.

The argument so far has focused on the local economy. It has suggested that there are features specific to the local apparatus of production and consumption that may create openings for intervention that can win popular support. Relatively modest measures aimed at shifting the local pattern of demand and supply may create important spaces. We might visualise the structure of the local economy — and the focus of a local strategy — in terms of a crude stratification:

1. Locally oriented sector (workers and employers in small firms, public sector).
2. Stimuli coming from non-local markets (local spending of workers and firms engaged in non-local sector).
3. Non-locally oriented sector (factories and offices located in the area).

The easiest, but mildest, measures involve altering the internal operation of the locally oriented sector, through expanding local demand or setting up new local suppliers of the kind suggested. The idea that a particular slice of economic activity can be fenced around may sound a little odd: just as there are lots of different ways in which a firm can respond to its market, so there are different ways in which a cluster of enterprises can respond. For example, if the dozens of marinas now being built around the coast of Wales were placed under coordinated local control they could channel the income they get in socially useful ways. The Mondragon experience at least makes that clear. A collective framework for control of the personal services and retail sectors could dramatically alter the way in which enterprises translate income into jobs. The scope for intervention at this level is conditioned by the stimulus coming from the non-local sector. At the moment the size of the non-local sector is subject to no popular control at all, and nor is the way it relates to the local sector. These two dimensions could, indeed must, become the targets for change if significant local gains are to be made.
   Even if the links between the local and non-local sector can be changed, there remains the problem that the non-local sector is very different in different places — the City is so wealthy that Covent Garden can prosper on its crumbs, but there's no real equivalent in Liverpool. If local demands increase, therefore, they must come up against the wider problem of the location of economic activity. This is the third 'layer' determining how much space for change there is locally. It follows that if really significant changes are to be won there has to be some way of controlling this layer. There is no alternative to creating new forms through which real control may be exerted over the location of factories and offices. Where such control is impossible the public sector alone will have to compensate with the way it locates its activities.
   The fact that the local economy is stratified means that the space available within each layer depends on different factors. At the most local level it depends on the behaviour of redistributive agencies such as local authorities, health authorities, and the ownership and control of local enterprises. At the level of the linkage to the non-local sector it depends on the internal organisation of production in non-localised firms. At the level of the overall proportions of the non-localised sector it depends on the way capital moves around nationally and internationally, and on the state.
   Traditionally, thinking about localities in socialist circles has

been confined to the third layer. Various proposals for the distribution of industry have been made — although usually very feeble ones. In recent years there have been some attempts to look at the second layer and authorities such as Wandsworth and later the GLC and West Midlands have explored ways of trying to change the interaction between firms and the locality. Many local authorities have pleaded for firms in their area to spend more locally. In some respects they have also experimented with modest interventions at the first level.

A new local politics aimed at creating space for local demands could add a whole new dimension to socialist strategy. Politicising the local economy could both lead to modest immediate gains and would raise new questions about control at higher levels. Specific notions of socially useful production could play an important part in helping to crystallise issues and mobilise protest. This could happen, of course, if new frameworks emerge to support local movements, which in turn will eventually generate new approaches to national and international questions.

This may seem a remote prospect, but things are changing very quickly. One of the most vivid lessons of Britain's attempts to devise a policy towards the regions and the inner cities is that nothing forces the state to react like the threat of trouble. In the 1980s there will be more trouble, but it is likely to be anarchic and chaotic and the state's response is likely to be increasingly repressive unless a new focus can be found. Politicising the local economy may help to provide such a focus. It can also provide a whole new basis for workers' plans to feed into wider strategies. Decline and poverty are being projected down to the local level right across the country. As Britain continues its slide to become the poorest ex-industrial nation in Europe, the materials of which local protest are made will accumulate in every town, affecting those out of work as much as those in it.

In 1983 the Tories effectively abolished democratic local government — or what was left of it. The Labour Party's response has been to lament the loss of its old stamping ground rather than to rethink the whole question of locality. The Alternative Economic Strategy is still pitched at the level of a centralised strategy for national recovery, with local issues added on as an opportunistic afterthought. It is time to look at ways of building a new decentralised popular strategy within which 'democratic forms and local and grassroots organisations must be the building blocks'. Without this, locality will remain an instrument for dividing working class people from each other, and 'socially useful production' will remain just another single issue.

PART THREE

Looking to the Future

CABLING WHOSE FUTURES?

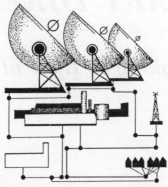

**Cable should not be seen as a further installation of public service broadcasting but as something different.
White Paper on Cable, Cmnd 8866, 1983**

However the development of cable in Britain works out, its potential is immense. Cable is a key part in the astonishing and highly profitable development of the communications and information industries. It could enable a far wider exchange of material between groups; it could facilitate a democratic right of access to information, quickly and in the home; it could lead to the sharing of new kinds of pleasure. In fact it is already clear that government policy is ruthlessly dedicated towards enormous advantages for a limited number of companies; and towards a significant widening of the information gap into a chasm. There will be those who know and can find out, and those who cannot buy or find a way into this privileged club. There will be very little democratic accountability; while some cable channels will create great difficulties for those trying to maintain a comprehensive broadcasting service. Two things stand out: that, once again, technology is not neutral; and that the Left as a whole is far behind in understanding these developments, let alone clarifying a socialist policy for them. Our lives may be transformed — but under capitalist auspices?

Timothy Hollins, *Beyond Broadcasting: Into the Cable Age* BFI 1984.
Brian Murphy, *The World Wired Up: Unscrambling the New Communications Puzzle* CoMedia 1983.
P. Golding and G. Murdock, 'Privatising Pleasure', *Marxism Today* October 1983.

CHAPTER TWELVE

Present Tense Technology
David Noble

Introduction

In three articles published in *Democracy* the distinguished American scholar, David Noble, examined the history and present position of 'direct industrial action — a refusal of new technologies which culminates in acts of sabotage and destruction. Such acts, when they are discussed at all, are usually dismissed as 'mindless violence'; unrealistic attempts to dam the flow of innovation and technological development. In other words, they are written off as mere Ludditism. But, in common with some other historians, Noble believes that the Luddites — far from being mindless wreckers of machines — were directly and consciously fighting back against early capitalism's attempt to deskill workers, lower labour costs, and impose new forms of supervision and control on workers. Clearly, such questions have not been effaced by time; they are the very questions with which Socially Useful Production projects are concerned today.

Noble argues that any contemporary resistance to the imposition of new technologies is seriously weakened by the fact that capital is armed not only with obvious power on a global scale, but also with less visible cultural and ideological power. A central component of this power is the fact that technology has been constructed as an innocent force whose imperatives spring from neutral, apolitical sources. Noble traces the main features of this construction back to the Industrial Revolution in order to remind us that *technology is political* and is shaped by determinate groups for particular ends.

In order to develop this point, Noble examines the role of intellectuals over the past 200 years in creating and sustaining theories of modernity, technology and progress which have supported the logic of capitalism. More importantly, he traces the transformation of such theories into a generally accepted 'common sense' which, being shared by all, has greatly weakened the analyses and actions of the opponents of capital's hegemony.

David Noble is writing from the perspective of North America, but his analysis transcends any particular national form of political and industrial action. From an examination of the way the Luddites 'shattered the illusion of the beneficence of the emerging capitalist order', he connects modern movements in the USA, Scandinavia, Germany and Britain with a history of opposition at the point of production which stretches back over 200 years. Perhaps the implied sense of continuity is too smooth, but it is important that the historical reach and potential contemporary power of such movements should be examined.

Most important, from the point of view of this book, is that Noble reminds us that Socially Useful Production is not only about creating jobs or experimenting with new relations of production. It is also central to a politics of refusal, resistance and the creation of alternatives. Such a politics would have to make a socialist view of technology together with democratic forms for the use of technology. This will only be done by connecting industrial, political and cultural forms of struggle.

What follows are selected quotations from all three articles. Noble's working of specific historical instances is often very fine and much of this is, of course, lost in our selection. However, we feel that the quotations, carrying as they do the main thrust of his argument, will be valuable as the starting point to a debate in this important area. The headings are our own and sections (sometimes quite long) edited out are indicated by (. . .).

* * *

The Power of Technology in the Class Struggle

There is a war on, but only one side is armed: this is the essence of the technology question today. On the one side is private capital, scientised and subsidised, mobile and global, and now heavily armed with military-spawned command, control, and communication technologies. Empowered by the second Industrial Revolution, capital is moving decisively now to enlarge and to consolidate the social dominance it secured in the first. In the face of a steadily declining rate of profit, escalating conflict, and intensifying competition, those who already hold the world hostage to their narrow interests are undertaking once again to restructure the international economy and the patterns of production to their advantage. Thus, with the new technology as a weapon, they steadily advance upon all remaining vestiges of worker autonomy, skill, organisation, and power in the quest for more potent vehicles of investment and exploitation. And, with the new technology as their symbol, they launch a multi-media cultural offensive designed to rekindle confidence in "progress". As their extortionist tactics daily diminish the wealth of nations, they announce anew the optimistic promises of technological deliverance and salvation through science. (. . .)

No one alive today remembers firsthand the trauma that we call the first Industrial Revolution, which is why people are now able so casually to contemplate (and misunderstand) the second. What little we actually know about those earlier times — perhaps the only adequate antecedent to our own — has filtered down to us through distorting lenses devised to minimise this calamity and justify the human suffering it caused in the name of progress. The inherited accounts of this period were formulated by and large in response to the dramatic actions of those who fought for their survival against this progress. They constituted a post hoc effort to deny the legitimacy and rationality of such opposition in order to guarantee the triumph of capitalism. The Luddites were not themselves confused by this ideological invention. They did not believe in technological progress, nor could they have since the alien idea was invented after them, to try to prevent their recurrence. In light of this invention, the Luddites were cast as irrational, provincial, futile, and primitive. In reality, the Luddites were perhaps the last people in the West to perceive technology in the present tense, and to act upon that perception. They smashed machines. (. . .) The Luddites who resisted the introduction of new technologies were not against technology *per se* but rather against the social changes that the new technology reflected and reinforced. Thus, the workers of Nottingham, Yorkshire, and Lancashire were not opposed to hosiery and lace frames, the gig mill and shearing frames, larger spinning jennies or even power looms. Rather, in a post-war period of economic crisis, depression, and unemployment much like our own, they were struggling against the efforts of capital to restructure social relations. (. . .) Thus, they were able to perceive the changes in the present tense for what they were, not some inevitable unfolding of destiny but rather the political creation of a system of domination that entailed their undoing. They were also able to act decisively — and not without success when measured in terms of a human lifetime — to defend their livelihood, freedom, and dignity.

But the way we evaluate Luddism today has not been shaped by the Luddites themselves. Instead we have inherited the views of those who opposed machine breaking and who succeeded in removing the technology question from the point of production, from the workers themselves, from the present that was the first Industrial Revolution. In the place of that traumatic reality, they constructed technological myths about the power of the past and the promise of the future. And in the light of these myths the courageous Luddites were made to seem mistaken, pathetic, dangerous, and insane.

Ideology and Technology

The plight of the workers, made all the more visible by their dramatic protest, shattered the illusion of the beneficence of the emerging capitalist order and discredited once and for all the notion that this society was a realm of shared values and human ends. It is thus not mere coincidence that at this same time society was "discovered" to be a thing apart from the people who comprised it, and that it had a logic of its own that was distinct from and dominated the purposes and aspirations of people. Society as a human artifact, a human endeavour, composed of people, was lost in the wake of capitalism, only to be reinvented as an automatic, self-regulating mechanism in which people were simply "caught up". The hard logic of the market and the machine surfaced supreme, replacing human inspiration, as Lewis Mumford observed, with "the abstractions of constant technological progress and endless pecuniary gain". Henceforth would "the belief in technological progress, as a good in itself, replace all other conceptions of desirable human destiny". Political notions of justice, fairness, freedom, equality, reason — the hallmarks of enlightened statecraft and the bourgeois revolutions themselves, now gave way to mechanical notions of social betterment. As capitalism revealed its inhuman core, its champions vanished, to be replaced by invisible hands. And social progress became identified with impersonal intermediaries: manufactures, industry, goods, machinery. As human society and people became variables (i.e., commodities, factors of production) capital became the constant, not alone the tangible sign of progress but also the imagined engine or cause of progress. And capitalism, opposed by the workers as a system of domination, exploitation, and alienation, now emerged as simply a system of production that was identified with progress itself. Such progress, moreover, was viewed as natural and necessary; social prosperity and human happiness would inevitably flow from this automatic process, so long as people allowed it to follow its own natural course, so long as they yielded to the requirements of free competition and untrammelled technological development. If *laissez-faire* became one manifesto of capitalism, *laissez-innover* became the other. "In my opinion, machinery ought to be encouraged to any extent whatsoever", wrote George Beaumont. Ultimately, he believed, such development would fulfill the dreams of the workers because the inventors of machinery were after all the "true benefactors of mankind".

This emergent ideology of technological progress served capitalist development well in the name of material prosperity, and diverted attention away from the exploitation entailed. At the same time, it shaped all subsequent critiques of capitalism. Even socialists, sworn enemies of capitalist aggrandisement and the profit system, were hereafter compelled to accommodate this new cultural contrivance, to adopt the faith in technological deliverance that had become hegemonic. (. . .)

And what political economy and the scientific movement failed to do, the true believers in the machine itself, the technical enthusiasts and mystics accomplished, attributing to machines the force of necessity itself. Thus Charles Babbage, inventor of one of the earliest computers, noted in the 1832 preface to his *Economy of Machinery and Manufactures*, that his book was but an application of the principles of his calculating engine to the factory system as a whole, to demonstrate the mathematical precision and predictability machine-based industry made possible. In the midst of the machine-breaking movement, Babbage contemplated the computer-run factory. At the same time, Andrew Ure, whose description of textile manufacturing served as Karl Marx's point of departure for a critique of modern industry, extolled the virtues of machinery for extending and ensuring total management-control over production (as the Luddites were understood). In Ure's mind, the factory took on "mystical qualities", as Berg puts it; he described the mill as a vast automaton, with all parts in concert, subordinated to the discipline of the self-regulating prime mover, the steam engine. And Ure's fantastic vision of the ultimate end of this new discipline, the fully automated factory, like Babbage's computer-run factory, pictured capitalist industry as the very embodiment of reason, against which worker opposition could not but appear to be futile and irrational. It was thus not the fantasists who were deemed lunatics but the quite realistic and all too level-headed workers who dared to stand in their way. (. . .)

The hegemonic ideology of technological progress, moreover,

left its mark on the developing workers' movement as its leaders struggled to be taken seriously in this new intellectual climate. For although they gained strength as a consequence of the workers' actions against machinery, the political champions of labour's cause were no more disposed to follow the workers' lead than were the apologists and agents of capital. They abandoned the workers' strategy not because it proved ineffective but because they believed they knew what was in the workers' best interest, and were becoming certain that opposition to technological progress was no part of it. (. . .)

The removal of the struggle from the point of production rendered matters of machinery and production secondary to the political issues that lay beyond the realm of actual production. One result of the political and ideological subordination of the workers by their leaders, then, was a minimisation of the matters the workers themselves initially considered central, and the elimination of the types of direct action that the workers themselves had found to be most effective in their fight against capital. And this diminished debate over and opposition to the introduction of machinery had the effect of ensuring the continued and strengthened hegemony of the doctrine of technological progress, as well as the capitalist system. (. . .)

The Second Industrial Revolution

Labour's response to the first Industrial Revolution set a pattern that was repeated in the wake of the second. Once again it was the workers immediately affected by the changes who first sounded the alarm, described the dangers, and undertook direct means to try to slow the assault on their jobs and lives. And once again the issue of technological change was expropriated from the workers by those who spoke for them. The issue was removed from the point of production to executive offices and research centres, where it was fitted into ideological and political agendas of future progress. The result was a loss not just of an understanding of the reality confronting workers but of a strategy for dealing with it — in the present.

What mechanisation was to the first Industrial Revolution, automation was to the second. The roots of the second Industrial Revolution lay in the state-sponsored technological developments of World War II. Military technologies — control systems for automatic gunfire, computers for ballistics and A-bomb calculations, microelectronics for proximity fuses, radar, computers, aircraft and missile guidance systems, and a host of sensing and measuring devices — gave rise to not only programmable machinery but also "intelligent" or self-correcting machinery. In the post-war years, the promotion of such technologies was fuelled by Cold War concerns about "national security", the enthusiasm of technical people, management's quest for a solution to its growing labour problems, and by a general cultural offensive to restore confidence in scientific salvation and technological deliverance following the twin traumas of depression and global war.

The late 1960s and early 1970s were marked by an outpouring of worker initiative, cynicism, and rage about union leadership collaboration, and a renewed emphasis upon direct action. (. . .) As workers fought to overcome their political subordination within their own organisations, their plight became more visible. And as they began to achieve their aim, the struggle against capital became less ideologically constrained and thus more direct and effective. As workers became sophisticated about the ways that the new integrated automation systems rendered management even more vulnerable to sabotage than before, new forms of direct action emerged and spread throughout the workforce, to the skilled and unskilled alike, young and old, unionised and non-unionised, men and women, veterans and new industrial workers, in all industries. (. . .)

As with the Luddite revolts of the first Industrial Revolution, resistance to the second Industrial Revolution was met with repression. People were disciplined, jailed, isolated, and otherwise intimidated. In 1970, for example, France passed a new law against "all instigators, organisers, or deliberate participants in sabotage". While using the upsurge to advantage at the bargaining table, the unions — liberal, social democratic, and communist alike — condemned much of the direct action and publicly distanced themselves from it.

Management responded to the wave of rank-and-file militancy with disciplinary measures, lock-outs, and legal devices, as well as by designing and introducing new technology that, it was hoped, would diminish the possibility of worker intervention in production or eliminate the need for workers altogether. In addition to these traditional responses, the managers of some companies experimented with new methods — so-called job enrichment, job enlargement, and quality-of-worklife schemes — designed to absorb discontent and redirect energies along more productive paths. Sweden was a centre for such experimentation and became a model throughout the industrialised world.

"Far from being motivated by a new co-operative attitude between labour and capital in Sweden", however, as auto-industry historian David Gartmann has noted, "these changes in technology and work [were] the results of renewed class struggle". Sweden too had been struck by an epidemic of worker rebellion and resistance even more severe than in the United States; absenteeism, labour turnover, and wildcat strikes had escalated dramatically. At Volvo, daily absenteeism had reached over 15 per cent and annual labour turnover peaked at over 50 per cent. "The main reason for such resistance", Gartmann noted, was "discontent with the stultifying, monotonous, and intense nature of the work itself", which was reinforced by the introduction of automation. P.G. Gyllenhammer, Volvo president at the time, acknowledged that "labour unrest that became visible in 1969 made it necessary to adapt production control to changing attitudes in the workforce".

In the United States, many companies also initiated job-enrichment schemes to try to regain the loyalty and co-operation of the workforce as well as to insure the fullest utilisation of expensive new equipment. Most of these experiments succeeded in terms of increasing productivity, output, and quality, and reducing absenteeism and turnover, but they were terminated once the workforce began to use their expanded responsibilities to try to extend further their control over production. (. . .)

Still building upon the energies unleashed by the workers themselves, the professionals soon produced a plethora of publications, conferences, and research, and assisted the trade unions in formulating new contract language and, ultimately, new agreements on the introduction of new technology. Whatever these gains, however, they were achieved at the expense of removing the technology issue from the shopfloor and thus from the realm of direct action available to the workers themselves. (. . .)

Reacting to the accelerating technological agenda of management — which has always used change as a tactic to disorient its opposition — the unions have been forced onto the defensive. Trying to hold on and keep track of (if not pace with) new developments, the unions have been forced to focus upon what is changing (technology) and to ignore what is not (the dominant relations of power). While this exercise in frenetic futility has done little to help the unions and their members find a way out of their predicament, it has provided a great deal of full-time work for researchers. Seduced into the details of the technology and endlessly documenting the horrors, they have intensified the trade union obsession with professional rather than worker competence and even lent a degree of polite respectability to the unions' futile efforts. Most important, they have reinforced a fundamental confusion about the social realities of technological development.

The Social Reality of Technology

The recognition that technology is political constituted an important ideological breakthrough since it overcame the fatalism of technological determinism, long a staple of capitalist apologetics. But there are at least two possible conclusions that could be drawn from this belated insight. First, the understanding that technology reflects power relations in society could imply that those with more power would continue to determine the shape and direction of technology for the foreseeable future. Therefore, the conclusion to be drawn would be twofold: in the long run to try to shift the balance of power, and in the short run to do everything possible to prevent the introduction of the present technology, since it reflects the interests of those in command. Those few who have experimented with this position have invariably stumbled upon the taboos against Luddism, the cultural compulsions of progress, and economic deterministic arguments about efficiency, productivity, and competitiveness. Thus, they have always opted for a formalistic approach and settled for bargaining over technology post hoc and from a position of weakness. There has been little evidence of any unions actually mobilising workers to try to increase their power *vis-à-vis* management and even less of any concerted attempt to organise opposition to the introduction of new technology. (. . .)

Confronted by this technology-based assault, battered by the economic recession, and confounded by its own (derived) commitment to technological progress, labour has been thrown on the defensive. In the process, unions have almost entirely abandoned the crucial struggles over technology and working conditions ignited by the rank-and-file rebellions of the late 1960s. Those workers who have continued to insist upon such shopfloor struggles have been dismissed by union officials intent upon maintaining dues-paying membership and keeping plants open, whatever the price in the present. Meanwhile, the "technology researchers" have abandoned even the pretense of dealing with the technologically-based challenges of the present, and have drifted ever more toward the development of technological alternatives for the future. However valuable all of this effort might some day prove to be, it is of little practical value to those now under immediate assault. Thus, in the face of an intensifying challenge, the capitulation of the unions, and the escapism of the experts, it is no wonder that workers in the shops have once again begun, increasingly, to take matters into their own hands. Having overcome the fatalism of technological determinism, they have now begun to overcome also the futurism of technological progress, and to shift attention back to the present. The resurgence of the rank and file, moreover signals the return as well of direct action at the point of production. (. . .)

If workers have begun to smash the physical machinery of domination, so responsible intellectuals must begin deliberately to smash the mental machinery of domination. They must strive to overcome — in themselves as well as in others — the collective fear of being human and free now reified and ratified as fixed ideas and solid-state circuitry. To do this, they must champion a new commonsense that insists without compromise upon the primacy of people's lives over the strange and estranging myths of automatic destiny. The intellectual task is one of recovery, reclamation, and reminders: of who and what we are and of what is being lost. (. . .) In line with the smashing of mental machinery, intellectuals must strive to overcome their own and others undue reverence for, and deference to, physical machinery, in order to develop criteria, defences, and devices for effective resistance to technological change. No one is against "technology", despite the frequently heard charge, because technology as such does not exist. Technology exists only in the particular, as particular pieces of equipment in particular settings. (. . .)

If opposition to technological progress helps us overcome our infantile dreams of technological salvation, it enables us also to transcend the technological mystification of power in our society. For technology has never really been the problem, nor will it ever be the solution. Technology does not by itself destroy democracy and neither does it bring democracy into being. If we have become a politically regressive society, it is not because of the politics of technology but because, "hypnotised" by ideologies of progress, we have substituted technology for politics. Ultimately, therefore, the real challenge posed by the current technological assault is for us to become able to put technology not simply in perspective but aside, to make way for politics. The goal must not be a human-centered technology but a human-centered society. And this demands, as it always has, a confrontation with power and domination.

These comments are drawn from a series of articles which appeared in *Democracy: A Journal of Political Renewal and Radical Change*, New York, during 1983.

CHAPTER THIRTEEN
Challenging Commoditisation — Producing Usefulness outside the Factory
Ursula Huws

'Production for Use, not Profit' has been a rallying slogan of socialists for many years. It seems an excellent, concise encapsulation of what a socialist industrial strategy should be, simultaneously exposing the unfeeling nature of capitalism and demonstrating the sensible, caring quality of socialism. It has an instant appeal to common sense.

Yet, unpicked a little, the demand turns out to conceal a puzzling underlying contradiction, which exemplifies much of the current confusion on the British Left about the direction an alternative economic and industrial strategy should take. For while it rejects the notion of profit as the over-riding drive force of change, as the ultimate criterion for whether or not a job should exist, it leaves unchallenged capitalism's favoured form of industrial activity, chosen precisely because it is the most efficient way of producing profit — commodity production. Built into the very form of the capitalist manufacturing production process is the subordination of all other factors to profit because it is only by manufacturing commodities for exchange that the capitalist can extract surplus value from the labour of his workforce.

The pre-eminence of commodity production has produced grotesque deformities in our industrial and economic development and brought into being many of the ugliest features of life under capitalism. It has meant that vast quantities of powdered cows' milk are available for babies, but there are no resources to educate their mothers to breast feed them; that the provision of drugs or medical equipment takes precedence over the supply of nurses; that it is easier to find a miniature Rolls Royce for a child than a nursery place; that we can equip old people with colour televisions more readily than we can give them warmth or friendship.

In an abstract, moralising way, socialists have long been

aware of the need for an alternative to this topsy turvy value system, variously labelled as 'materialism' or 'consumerism', and have devoted much rhetoric to attacking it, generally in a tone of sentimental regret for the lost warmth of 'close-knit' working class communities before the Second World War. Yet when they come to the business of devising concrete plans for the future, the emphasis is firmly on alternative *products*. Although factory work is widely regarded as monotonous, deskilled, degraded and dangerous, the solution proposed to the closing of factories is to reopen them or build new ones, not to think of alternatives to the factory system altogether. Why is it that the Left seems so reluctant to step outside capitalism's fixation with commodities? Why is the present socialist challenge to the primacy of profit so half-hearted and ambiguous?

A cluster of different, but related, factors seems to be involved: the sexual division of labour which relegates women to the 'service' jobs and perceives factory work as male; narrow and distorted definitions of skill which are the products of defensive struggles to sustain 'craft' wage rates rather than any rational analysis of job content; a blind faith in science and technology as neutral heralds of a progress which will ultimately be beneficial to all; a belief that working class consciousness and militancy are the exclusive preserve of operatives directly involved in the commodity manufacturing process.

These attitudes have deep historical roots. Before going on to examine how justified they are, it may be a useful exercise to begin unearthing some of these roots, to see how they have come about and what their relationship is to the reality of the production process.

Historical Roots of the Production Process

One starting point for this exercise, and the one adopted here, is to look at the processes by which various activities have become 'commoditised' over the past three centuries of capitalist development, and the effects that these processes have had on labour both within and without the cash nexus. It may then be possible to predict some future developments and plan strategies for intervention.

We are accustomed to a view of the economy which sees it as divided into distinct and separate sectors. There is the primary sector, consisting of agriculture, mining and quarrying, in which raw materials are extracted from the earth; there is the secondary, manufacturing sector, in which they are turned into commodities; and there is the tertiary, or 'service' sector, which comprises various state and commercial activities as well as a variety of distributive functions. In addition to these three sectors of the money economy there is a fourth group of activities, integral to their proper functioning but not involving waged labour. This has been called by a number of different names, none of them entirely satisfactory to my mind: the sphere of reproduction; consumption; domestic labour. It includes a variety of tasks carried out in the home and the community connected with the consumption of goods and services, with caring for the young, the old and the disabled, and with servicing the waged labour force. These tasks are predominantly carried out by women and, for the purposes of this chapter, will be termed 'unsocialised labour'.

It is generally assumed that these four sectors of the economy are both discrete and constant, separated absolutely from each other by easily-defined and unchanging boundaries, and these divisions are reflected in practices ranging from the routine collection of labour statistics to the formulation of political strategy. Whether it is the extreme Right of the Tory Party arguing that 'we cannot continue to consume more than we produce' or the socialist Left bemoaning the 'erosion of Britain's industrial base', the underlying assumption is the same, that it is possible to separate and counterpose the 'productive' manufacturing sector and the 'unproductive' services.

It thus requires quite a wrench to adjust to the recognition that the boundaries between these sectors are not only extremely blurred, but are also dynamic. Underneath the apparently static surface portrayed in the official statistics, there is constant movement with shifts and upheavals which profoundly affect all our lives.

At the micro level, that of the individual worker, it is easy enough to point to the blurring between sectors. A farm worker is mending his tractor — a 'primary' activity. He fails and has to call in a service engineer to do the same job. Immediately it's reclassified as 'tertiary'. A typist is typing the manuscript of a book, and thus productively employed in manufacturing. She is made redundant and re-employed in the civil service where the 'books' she types are official reports, and she's become an unproductive service worker. The man carrying newly completed stainless steel forks across the factory floor is in manufacturing; the woman carrying them across the shop is in services. From accountants to lorry drivers to cleaners there are many large groups of workers whose classification is essentially an arbitrary by-product of the size and degree of specialisation of their employers and whether or not there is a policy of subcontracting work.

While anomalies such as these serve a useful purpose in warning against over-reliance on the available data, they tell us little about major shifts in the boundaries between sectors. To see these, we need a broad historical overview. Any summary of the past 300 years of capitalist development in a few paragraphs like these is bound to be crude and simplistic. Nevertheless, it seems worth attempting for the light it sheds on the transformation of services into goods, and of unsocialised labour into paid work and back again.

At the beginning of this period, the manufacturing sector as it is today hardly existed. Many of the activities which now take place in factories, as well as a number of those now labelled 'services' took place in the home. As Alice Clark described it in *The Working Life of Women in the 17th Century* (1919):

> "In the seventeenth century it (the domestic role) embraced a much wider range of production: for brewing, dairy work, the care of poultry and pigs, the production of vegetables and fruit, spinning flax and wool, nursing and doctoring, all formed part of domestic industry".[1]

The range of goods produced in the home was immense, covering such items as soap, candles and medicines as well as food and clothing.

The first major production activity to move out of the home was textile manufacture, which, in the first factories, brought into being a new class of wage-earning workers.

As the factory gates began to be established, and waged work outside the home was created for women, the effect was not, as one might expect, to enrich the household by providing a source of income with which the new, factory-made goods could be purchased, but to impoverish it. To quote Alice Clark again,

> "If the father earned enough money to pay the rent and a few other necessary expenses, the mother could and did feed and clothe herself and her children by her own labours when she possessed enough capital to confine herself wholly to domestic industry. The value of a woman's productive capacity to her family was, however, greatly reduced when, through poverty, she was obliged to work for wages, because then, far from being able to feed and clothe her family, her wages were barely adequate to feed herself".

It seems to have been necessity, in the form of a shortage of time and financial resources, which fuelled the choice to become a consumer of manufactured goods rather than to continue to produce them in the home. The new class of factory workers were also obliged by their lack of time and inadequate accommodation to become purchasers of services, a prerogative hitherto restricted to those rich enough to employ domestic servants. This gave rise to a new range of 'service' occupations such as childminding, taking in washing, purveying cooked foods, some of which were later to become the basis of major new industries.

Accompanying this development was a continuing growth of the professional services which had already begun to oust some of the functions previously carried out voluntarily in the community by wise women and respected elders — the fee-charging surgeons and apothecaries, doctors and lawyers, the replacement of oral traditions of education by literary ones.

Thus far, we have seen a movement of some activities out of the sphere of unsocialised labour and into that of manufacturing, and of others out of unsocialised labour and into that of services. But there is another type of movement which became increasingly important over the succeeding centuries — a movement from services into manufacturing. To illustrate some of these changes with concrete examples, two charts have been devised (see over page). These show in a highly schematic and drastically simplified form, what has happened to four sets of activities, almost exclusively carried out in the home in the 17th Century, over the ensuing 300 years. The four household activities chosen are washing clothes, caring for the sick, entertaining and preparing food, but their selection is fairly arbitrary. They could easily be replaced with others such as supplying heat or light, passing on news, making clothes or cleaning. Reading the charts horizontally, we can follow the progress of these activities through various different stages.

The left-hand column gives a broad summary of the situation in the home before the industrial revolution, when these were domestic tasks mainly carried out by women for the use of the immediate household. The second column shows how many of these functions became transformed into paid, sometimes 'professional' services which, although they may have already existed embryonically long before the industrial revolution, began to become widespread with the growth of wage-earning. In order for these tasks to move outside the home there was no necessity for the way in which they were carried out to change. The technology and work process could remain identical, the only alteration necessitated being one of social relations — the performers of the tasks were now carrying out the service for money, not for the use of themselves or their families.

The next stage, however, required the intervention of science

ENTERTAINING

17th Century → **Late 20th Century**

TECHNOLOGY
Sound and vision recording and transmission techniques. Electronics, cable, satellites etc.

UNSOCIALISED LABOUR	SERVICE SECTOR	MANUFACTURING SECTOR	UNSOCIALISED LABOUR
Entertaining. Singing, story-telling, performing with musical instruments, dancing etc.	Professional performing in bands, orchestras, circuses, music-halls etc. Later projectionists, usherettes etc. in cinema.	Factory production of radios, records, TVs, hi-fi systems, VTRs and associated accessories.	'Self-service' entertainment — purchasing or renting hardware and software.

LABOUR PROCESS

Fairly high general level of skills and knowledge required.	High specialised level of skills and knowledge required.	A few highly-specialised jobs requiring advanced skill and knowledge. Majority of jobs unskilled.	Low skill-levels in operation of equipment, but bring cultural and other knowledge to TV, music, food etc.
Worker controls pace of work.	Worker has some control of pace of work.	Most workers have no control over pace of work.	Worker has some control over the order of tasks.
Entire work process and its hazards known and understood.	Most of work process known and understood.	Little of work process known or understood. Unknown hazards.	Little knowledge of how machines or products work.

UNSOCIALISED LABOUR	SERVICE SECTOR	MANUFACTURING SECTOR	UNSOCIALISED LABOUR
Food preparation in subsistence agriculture, every stage from planting to consumption is based in the home.	Domestic service and a large variety of specialised jobs in shops — from master pastrycook to delivery boy.	Factory preparation of food and production of cookers, freezers, mixers and other appliances.	Self-service selection of prepared foods; transport and storage; purchase, maintenance, operation of appliances.

TECHNOLOGY
Chemical industry; canning, freezing and preserving techniques; engineering technology. Genetic engineering.

FOOD PREPARATION

WASHING

17th Century → Late 20th Century

TECHNOLOGY
chemical industry; mechanical and electronic engineering.

UNSOCIALISED LABOUR
Care of personal and household fabrics including washing, ironing, starching, soap-making, dry cleaning, etc.

SERVICE SECTOR
Domestic service and out-work. Paid work 'taking in washing' and laundry work.

MANUFACTURING SECTOR
Factory production of soap, detergents, etc; washing machines, dryers etc.

UNSOCIALISED LABOUR
Buying, operating, maintaining appliances. If poor, going to launderette.

LABOUR PROCESS
Fairly high general level of skills and knowledge required.
Worker controls pace of work.
Entire work process and its hazards known and understood.

High specialised levels of skills and knowledge required.
Worker has some control of pace of work.
Most of work process known and understood.

A few highly-specialised jobs requiring advanced skill and knowledge. Majority of jobs unskilled.
Most workers have no control over pace of work.
Little of work process known or understood. Unknown hazards.

Low skill-levels (literacy to read instructions). Knowledge of brand-name, prices.
Worker has some control over the order of tasks.
Little knowledge of how machines or products work.

UNSOCIALISED LABOUR
Caring for the sick; growing and preparing herbs; bone-setting; midwifery etc.

SERVICE SECTOR
Doctors, nurses, pharmacists and ancillary services.

MANUFACTURING SECTOR
Factory production of drugs and medical and surgical appliances; diagnostic computers.

UNSOCIALISED LABOUR
First aid, buying proprietory medicines; transport of sick people to and from clinics etc. Waiting.

TECHNOLOGY
Drugs industry; mechanical and electronic engineering; other scientific developments.

CARING FOR THE SICK

and technology in order to take place. This was the transformation of these activities into manufacturing ones, their 'commoditisation', as one might call it. The boxes above and below each chart show some of the technological developments which were to affect these functions, and the third column illustrates the new manufacturing industries which were to grow up partly as a result of these developments, supplanting the old home-based manufacturing techniques and creating entirely new products. Finally, the fourth column gives a summary of what goes on in the present-day home, where these new products, and the new services which they in turn engender, are consumed.

Despite the very great differences between the four different functions illustrated in the chart, the overall pattern of development emerges as remarkably similar. The functions are initially socialised mainly as services which, as a result of technological change, are then commoditised to provide the basis for new manufacturing industries. The existence of these new commodities in turn alters the consumption patterns of the mass of the population, transforming the nature of the remaining unsocialised labour.

It would be wrong, of course, to imply that this development is a smooth and consistent one. It has come about through a series of unsteady jolts, with long periods during which several stages of development exist alongside each other. However since 'service' methods of production are almost invariably more labour-intensive than 'manufacturing' ones, they inevitably become progressively more and more expensive in relation to the purchase of commodities as mass production gets underway, and tend to dwindle into insignificance.

Jonathan Gershuny[2] has done pioneering research on this process whereby services are ousted by goods. His work gives us concrete information on the extent and time-scale of such change, and demonstrates conclusively that, although invisible in conventionally assembled statistics, it is a sweeping trend with far-reaching implications. For instance, in one 20-year period there was a complete turning upside down of the relationship between consumption of services and goods in three areas: the substitution of commodity-based home entertainment for cinema and theatre-going, the use of domestic appliances instead of laundry services and domestic help and of cars and motor bikes instead of public transport. The accompanying table shows the extent of this substitution expressed as a percentage of the total UK budget. If one takes account of the fact that during this period the cost of the manufactured goods fell in real terms while the cost of services increased, then the changeabout was even greater than is apparent from these figures.

The substitution of goods for services 1954-1974

Some selected expenditure categories	Percentage of total UK budget				
	1954	1961	1966	1971	1984
Cinemas, theatres etc.	2.0	1.0	1.0	0.6	0.8
Television: buy and rent	1.4	2.1	2.1	2.3	3.0
Domestic help and laundry	1.6	1.2	1.1	0.8	0.8
Domestic appliances	0.8	1.7	1.4	1.5	1.7
Transport services	3.5	3.1	3.2	2.9	2.4
Transport goods	3.5	7.2	8.6	10.8	11.1

Source: Jonathan Gershuny, *After Industrial Society? The Emerging Self-Service Economy*, Macmillan, 1978.

In the 17th Century, as mentioned above, a crucial factor in the choice to buy goods or services rather than produce them in the home was the shortage of time. It would be reasonable to expect that there would continue to be a direct relationship between the growth of socialised labour and reductions in time spent on unsocialised work — the more goods and services for household consumption produced, the less time needed to be spent on housework.

The available evidence on time spent on domestic labour is scant. While there are many accounts of the backbreaking toil involved in housework and its never-ending quality, there are to my knowledge no reliable estimates of the total number of hours devoted to it by the servantless classes in the 18th and 19th centuries. Even in the 20th Century, the surveys are few on the ground. In 1974, Ann Oakley[3] summarised the studies which she had managed to identify (see over page).

Astonishingly enough, according to this evidence, during a period when there was an unprecedented and spectacular proliferation of domestic appliances, household chemicals, speedy forms of transport, and other 'labour saving' commodities, the time spent on housework actually went *up*.

Several factors appear to have contributed to this unlikely phenomenon. Firstly, there have been powerful ideological pressures, vividly analysed by Barbara Ehrenreich and Deirdre English[4] which have forced up the standards of housework and created new tasks even as the work itself has become simpler. Secondly, the small nuclear household does not lend itself to

Time spent on housework increases, despite the spread of 'labour saving' devices

Study	Date	Average weekly hours of housework
1. **Rural studies**		
United States	1929	62
United States	1929	64
United States	1956	61
France	1959	67
2. **Urban Studies**		
United States	1929	51
United States (small city)	1945	78
United States (big city)	1945	81
France	1948	82
Britain	1950	70
Britain	1951	72
France	1958	67
Britain	1971	77

Source: Ann Oakley, *Housewife*, Penguin, 1974.

economies of scale, which means that automation cannot bring with it the quantum leaps in productivity associated with its introduction into industry.

There is, however, a third factor, and it is this above all which concerns us here. The commoditisation of services described above has had the effect of creating new types of unpaid 'consumption' work. It could in fact be said to have *de*socialised many labour processes which previously constituted part of paid employment.

In shops, for example, the consumer has taken over many of the tasks of goods selection, transport, weighing, packing and waiting which used to be carried out by paid assistants. Self-service has also become the norm in such services as petrol stations, cash dispensing and cafeterias. In the health service, it is no longer usual for doctors and nurses to visit patients in their own homes. It has been discovered that their (paid) time can be saved if users of the service can be persuaded to devote their (unpaid) time to travelling to and waiting in clinics and outpatients' departments of hospitals. Where computerised diagnostic systems have been installed the patients also take over many of the tasks previously performed by admissions clerks and nurses, feeding their own details into the information system. A similar process has taken place in many other service industries.

There is also additional labour involved in servicing and using many of the new privately-owned commodities, although this is often masked by the apparently greater ease and convenience of owning your own machine rather than relying on a public provision which has become expensive and unreliable. It is, for instance, more time-consuming to do washing even with an automatic machine than it was to use a laundry service which collected from and delivered to one's own front door.

Processes such as these represent yet another shift in the boundaries between socialised and unsocialised labour. The traffic between the private sphere of the home and the public one of the cash economy can now be seen to be two-way. As more and more activities are pulled out of the home and socialised on the one hand, the interests of forcing up productivity and shedding as many unprofitable tasks as possible in the outside economy are thrusting back onto the consumer other tasks which add to the burden of unpaid labour.

The processes of socialisation and commoditisation can thus be seen to have radically transformed the relationships between services and manufacturing industries and between paid and unpaid work during the last 300 years. What has happened to the labour process during this period?

Changes in the Labour Process

The charts which summarise the changing relationships between different sectors of the economy also include a simplified indication of some of the changes in the nature of the work carried out. It also highlights those variables which would appear to have most bearing on the quality of the work and the satisfaction to be gained from it from the point of view of the worker: skill, knowledge, control of the pace of work and an understanding of the dangers involved which, in combination with a degree of control over the work process, can help to safeguard a workers' health and safety.

In the 17th Century household we find an extremely wide spread of tasks, with seasonal variety, which, even allowing for an internal division of labour, demanded a broad range of skills from the workers. Most tasks were carried out from start to finish within the home, so all participants would have had an understanding of the total process and a high general level of knowledge of such things as cooking, curing meat, preserving methods, preparation of medical remedies, textiles, brewing, the manufacture of candles and soap, the care of animals and so on. While many individuals were undoubtedly overworked and bullied, the pace of work must have been determined informally or by group pressure when not controlled by the individual except in exceptional circumstances.

Turning to the service industries, we find an enormously diverse range of types of work. Drastic oversimplification is necessary in order to summarise them. But it would seem fair to say that, compared on the one hand with unsocialised labour and on the other with manufacturing industry, it is possible to identify a characteristic type of 'service' job. This is one in which the range of skills and knowledge is not so wide as in the unsocialised household work of the 17th Century, but there is a greater degree of specialisation, resulting in a number of highly skilled occupations developing, dedicated to one particular type of task. In medicine, for example, the 'all-rounder' of the informal economy is replaced first by specialist pharmacists, surgeons, midwives and later by physiotherapists, gynaecologists, ophthalmologists and a host of other specialists. This increasing division of labour also resulted in specialist positions being created which do not involve such high levels of skill. These are mainly manual jobs such as cleaning, carrying messages or delivering goods, positioned at the bottom of the hierarchies which quickly developed in these new industries, but with some worker knowledge of the work process as a whole. Most involve interaction with people and forms of supervision and work pacing is humanly- rather than machine-determined. Many service industries have also provided some form of progression, with the possibility for workers to work their way up from subordinate to more senior positions. The combination of a high degree of specialised knowledge and a low level of automation has meant that most work hazards have been well understood, making avoidance relatively easy.

In manufacturing, the situation is very different. From Engels to Braverman commentators have described the changes that the factory system has made to work processes. While these changes have not come about all at once, and have often been met with fierce resistance from the workers, the overall tendency has been inexorably in one direction — the incorporation of as much of the skill content and control of the work as possible into machines and systems and the rendering of the vast majority of workers into an undifferentiated, unskilled, interchangeable mass. In relation to skills, a dual process takes place: on the one hand the creation of a few extremely highly skilled controlling and designing positions which require specialist knowledge, and on the other the development of a larger number of repetitive jobs each involving carrying out one small fragmented part of the production process. The gulf between the two is unbridgeable. Most workers now lack any overall view of the process and can only fully understand their own small part of it. The chemicals with which they must work, the computerised control systems and the other products of a mystified 'science' have been made incomprehensible to them, which means that their hazards cannot be understood either. Often, it is only when workers begin dying that any suspicion arises as to their dangers. Work is paced by machines, taking from the individual worker not only the power to pace the speed of the job but even, very often, the ability to argue about it with a human supervisor.

The final columns in the charts outline the nature of the work which goes on in the contemporary home. The basic functions are, of course, very similar to those carried out in homes three centuries earlier — the production and rearing of children and ensuring that members of the household are adequately fed, washed and clothed. However the manner in which these functions are carried out is vastly different. In fact, on analysis, it turns out to bear more resemblance to the labour process in manufacturing industry than it does to that in the 17th Century home. It is overwhelmingly based on the purchase, servicing and use of various commodities such as processed food, household chemicals, domestic appliances and manufactured clothes. The design and working method of most of these are not understood and the housewife must depend on the advice of 'experts' (usually in the form of fine-printed instructions) for information on how to use them and what their hazards might be. In the event of any breakdown or accident she is instructed to contact another expert — the repair man or a doctor — and must helplessly wait until they have put the matter to rights (if, indeed, they are capable of doing so).

The housewife does have some control over the order in which she carries out tasks within the tight time structures dictated by school, work, shop opening hours and other external timetables, but the tasks which she must carry out and the standards to which she must comply in doing them are increasingly determined by the design of machines and houses, the chemical composition of food-mixes or fabrics, legal constraints (such as laws governing when children may be left with others or schooled) and strong ideological pressures. All of these mitigate against any real control of the work process. These processes have also removed most of the skill from housework, incorporating it, as in the case of factory workers, into the design of machinery. Ann Oakley quotes a comparative study of housewives with assembly-line and other factory workers, looking at three stress-producing factors in the nature of the work: monotony, fragmentation and speed. Despite the fact that they were subjected to none of the overt supervisory discipline of the factory floor, the housewives actually had a higher score on every count than manufacturing workers.

The Quality of Housework: comparison with factory work

Workers	*Percentage experiencing:*		
	Monotony	*Fragmentation*	*Speed*
Housewives	75	90	50
Factory workers	41	70	31
Assembly-line workers	67	86	36

Source: Ann Oakley, *op.cit.*

Far from liberating women from housework, then, we can see that the increasing commoditisation of household and service activities has had the opposite effect, transforming it into stressful drudgery. It has had a very similar effect on factory work, each wave of automation eliminating more and more skill and satisfaction from the work. The development of information technology has also had the effect of commoditising large areas of service employment, not only creating new manufacturing industries but also spreading some of the social relations of the factory into the office, shop, hospital and bank. Fragmentation and machine-pacing are now becoming characteristics even of some service jobs.

Barriers to Wider Thinking

In this knowledge, how can socialists argue uncritically for more commoditisation as a way of creating worthwhile jobs and a better society? Do they really believe that it is more pleasant to work in an electronic-alarm factory than to sit and talk to a frightened old lady? Or to stand at a conveyor belt making trolleys than help her carry her shopping? Is it really less rewarding to be a hospital porter or a nurse than a packer in a drug factory? And which of these jobs has the most potential for change, for transforming the social relations within an industry to give workers more involvement and control in their daily work?

As I observed at the beginning, there appear to be several barriers in socialist thinking to developing strategies which challenge the primacy of commodity production. The first of these is the sexual division of labour. In the unsocialised labour sector, it is overwhelmingly women who carry out the work of consumption, running the home and servicing the family. In the money economy, women are concentrated in relatively few industries and even fewer occupational groups. Apart from transport and defence, men are in a minority in all the service industries, which tend thus to be seen as female, while they dominate all the other industries with the exception of clothing and footwear (an industry which is fairly closely associated with unpaid activities carried out by women in the home). Women also have a substantial minority presence in the food and drink industries, electrical engineering and textiles, where they tend to be concentrated in certain clearly designated 'women's' jobs, but elsewhere they are hardly present at all except as clerical workers or cleaners. Perhaps precisely because they are responsible for unpaid work in the home, women's time is not regarded as valuable and these sharply differentiated areas where they work are generally also ghettoes of low pay.

Closely associated with this phenomenon is a devaluing of women's skills. A number of skills such as cleaning, cooking, childcare or making clothes are expected to be part of the normal equipment of every woman, who will, it is assumed, exercise them without reward for the good of her family in the home. They thus have no scarcity value whatsoever, so that when they come to be exchanged in the marketplace for wages the price they fetch is rock-bottom. In fact they are frequently not regarded as skills at all and those whose livelihood depends on them are generally labelled 'unskilled'.

The question of how skills are to be defined is confused and emotionally-charged, as Cynthia Cockburn has so brilliantly pointed out in her book, *Brothers*.[5] Frequently, the designation 'skilled' attached to a job is not so much a reflection of the intrinsic difficulty of performing it as of the degree of organisation and bargaining power of its holder. A central plank of the resistance of workers to the degradation and fragmentation of factory work has been the protection of past practices by labelling them 'skilled' and controlling access to them through the creation of apprenticeship schemes and the like. One explicit purpose of these craft groupings has been to resist dilution by more vulnerable groups of workers such as women and immigrants whose presence might weaken their bargaining power and unity, thus perpetuating and reinforcing the division of labour referred to above.

These practices have led to an identification of jobs done by women with low status. Most 'service' jobs are regarded as menial and degrading, if not effeminate, not so much because of their intrinsic nature (it is often extraordinarily arbitrary which jobs have become seen as 'male' and which 'female') but because they have taken on the attributes ascribed to those who normally carry them out.

Alongside this distorted evaluation of the relative value of different types of employment there is on the Left a stereotyped view of worker militancy. It is very difficult to shake off the idea that because it is the factory system which creates a class-conscious proletariat it must therefore be here that the strong workers' organisations will emerge which will bring capitalism to its knees. Leaving aside the role of peasants in Russia, China, Cuba and other countries which have experienced revolutions, we need look no further than British history to see what a dubious notion this is. By far the most powerful political force in the British labour movement in this century has been the so-called triple alliance of dockers, miners and transport workers. Not one of these groups is involved in commodity production. The miners are involved in primary sector extraction and the other two are designated 'services'. All three are however male, which may partly explain the fact that they are not generally perceived as such. Not so the workers who brought down the Callaghan government in the 'winter of discontent' in 1978. These were largely female public sector service workers. It is difficult to point to any group of manufacturing workers whose actions have had such great political effects, although it is certainly true that many have shown great militancy in pursuit of their aims as compared with some service workers. This would appear to be, however, not so much a product of their different relation to capital but of their gender.

Women service workers find it harder to organise not because they are service workers but because they are women: they cannot attend meetings because of household commitments; they are obliged to work part-time or for small firms which are near where they live; they are excluded, patronised or harassed by men; or because their economic need is too desperate to hold out for the best wages and conditions. These three factors are closely connected. Together, they give us a stereotype of the working class militant as a white, male, factory worker whose work is somehow ennobling. As the only 'real producer of wealth' his labour is not only seen as important and dignified but also as skilled and as providing some sort of a model for how all work should be in a future socialist society. By contrast other work — generally in services — is considered servile and undignified, if not downright parasitic. It is also perceived as unskilled and womanish, not fit employment for a real man.

Statistics show that the real composition of the working class contradicts this image in a number of ways. Over 40 per cent of workers are women, for instance, and an even higher proportion of workers is employed in service occupations. But it also sits uneasily with socialist ideology at a more abstract level. For we are, are we not, committed to trying to create a more caring society? And if caring is to be socialised, then what does it consist of but services? And how are we to fit this boiler-suited male factory worker into such a vision? The resolution of this contradiction is no simple matter, and must have exercised quite a few minds on the Left over recent years. It is this dilemma which must explain the delight with which so many have seized on the idea of the alternative, socially useful product. For if such products can be identified, then these workers can be put back into their factories and carry on exercising their skills while also producing the use values which people need. They can show they care without ever having to contaminate their manhood by actually entering into a service relationship with the needy.

Such a solution also conforms with another idea which is commonly held among Marxists and which reinforces the idea that more and more commodity production is the way forwards to a socialist future. This is the notion that science and technology are neutral forces of progress which must be developed as rapidly as possible so that, when the time is ripe, they can be appropriated by the working class under whose ownership they will produce leisure and plenty for all. In the past few years a critique of this idea has grown up, in this country led by the women's movement and groups like the British Society for Social Responsibility in Science. Together with some trade unionists, ecologists, peace groups and people involved in alternative health practices they have developed a convincing analysis which portrays capitalist science and technology as fundamentally distorted. The technology is developed for destruction not construction, it is anti-woman and anti-worker in its conception and design and could not be taken over in its existing form without continuing to pose an enormous threat to life, health and control of daily life. The science is mystified and irrelevant, its priorities dictated by the class which pays for and directs its progress. This critique gives us further grounds for caution in the face of the idea that more commodity production will necessarily take us a step towards socialism.

*   *   *

What, then, is the way forward? It is obviously untrue to suggest that there was a pre-technological golden age in the past during which people's lives were pleasant and healthy, and to which we should seek to return. New technology has always had contradictory effects and has eliminated many evils, even while it has created new ones. The process of commoditisation is not in and of itself necessarily against the interests of the working class as a whole, or of women within it. However it seems to me that it needs to be questioned much more carefully than it has been in the past by socialists.

When devising strategies for the future which seek simultaneously to create jobs and to meet social need, the starting point should not be the assumption that a product will necessarily be the answer. If it is then, in all probability, forces already at work within capitalism will find it. On the contrary, we should start from an analysis of the unmet need, which means listening to the views put forward by the needy themselves through their own organisations. Do childbearing women really want more foetal monitors, or would they rather simply have more, and differently trained midwives? Do the severely disabled want new gadgets, or would they prefer more money, more home helps, or differently designed houses? What labour does housework actually consist of, and how could it best be socialised? Can we reverse the trend towards a more capital intensive service sector and the self-service economy? And how can work processes be redesigned to make them safer and more satisfying? Some of these questions may produce answers which suggest that new commodities are needed, but it is likely that a great many will not.

If we are to produce solutions which meet these needs without creating new ghettoes of poorly paid low-status work, then a number of cherished ideas must be challenged, and new ways of organising developed. In particular socialists must begin to question the sexual and racial division of labour and find ways to overcome it, and begin to make it a priority to listen to and help organise groups which have traditionally been silent and isolated, in the community and in the unionised parts of the service sector.

References

1. Clark, Alice, *The Working Life of Women in the 17th Century*, 1919, George Routledge & Sons.
2. Gershuny, Jonathan, *After Industrial Society: The Emerging Self-Service Economy*, 1978, Macmillan.
3. Oakley, Ann, *Housewife*, 1974, Penguin Books.
4. Ehrenreich, Barbara and English, Deirdre, *For Her Own Good*, 1979, Pluto Press.
5. Cockburn, Cynthia, *Brothers*, 1983, Pluto Press.

Some of the ideas in this chapter first appeared in a different form in a paper written for a seminar at the South Bank Polytechnic in 1982.

CHAPTER FOURTEEN

Socially Useful Production and the Unemployed
Cliff Allum and Vin McCabe

In a time when the ideology of conservatism and capitalism in its Western form seems not only dominant but on the offensive in Britain, it is perhaps particularly important to clarify and promote the notion of production for social need and make such a demand relevant, and seem so, to working people throughout the country. And by 'working people', we do *not* mean simply those (un)lucky enough to be wage workers in our recession bound society, but also those performing unpaid domestic labour and/or those who are unable to secure employment.

Socially useful production, with its analytic origin in Marx's distinction between use value and exchange value, implies a reversal of capitalist logic. It asserts that use-value dominates, rather than is dominated by, exchange value. Theoretically, this means the production of goods and services outside of market constraints. However, current discussions about socially useful production very often concern alternatives within capitalism itself. In our view this has led to the development of two related components of socially useful production: one concerning the idea of this approach as an effective alternative, the other its practical implementation.

There seems some inherent confusion over the value-loaded term 'socially-useful products' which poses them as something capitalism cannot deliver. Marx argued that all goods and services necessarily have use value; it is just that they are produced because they make a profit, rather than because they are socially useful. Many workers, employed in capitalist firms, *are* making socially useful products. In some ways this represents a real limit to the 'alternative product' view of socially useful production. Further, to argue the predominance of use-value is also to argue an imperative that some form of organisation is necessary to promote socially-useful production which operates outside of immediate market parameters for wage-labour. This might be found in different directions: in individual (or 'co-operative') commodity production, or in local or national state planning, And it is the local state which has come particularly to the fore in recent years, notably in the notion of 'popular planning' itself.

The issue that we want to address in our contribution to this book concerns just how far the notion of socially useful production is relevant to people who are unemployed — don't these 'alternatives' exist primarily for those already at work?

Our discussion is in two parts. First we want to begin with some analysis of what unemployment really means and the nature of the 'traditional' Left responses, and then to identify what 'popular planning' commonly seems to be about. In the second part, we want to indicate some practical examples of areas of work in which we are involved and how these relate to popular planning.

The Nature of Unemployment

Unemployment is effectively a denial on two fronts. In the first place, someone who is unemployed ceases to contribute to the direct production of surplus value (or labour) — although they may find themselves as part of an unpaid army involved in the reproduction of labour power (the means by which wages are held down and workers' control limited). Employers are also denied the opportunity of exploiting this labour power for increased surplus value, although they may replace it by a technology which in turn increases unemployment within the workplace. Secondly, the ex-worker is cut off from the exchange of her/his labour for a wage and thus has no access to the main way in which wealth is redistributed in our society. S/he is denied access to the 'normal' channels of distribution within capitalism, and the problem of resources is consequently posed. Within British capitalism, the state, through the traditions of economic planning and welfare has intervened in both of these areas: in the first through the subsidies paid to private industry, sometimes directly linked to employment (e.g. the young workers scheme now currently in use), but more usually in a general form aimed at sustaining particular companies or industries in particular localities; in the second, by the establishment of a benefits system which provides some 'pay' for many people who are unemployed and thus takes on a distributional role.

Why are we setting out the discussion in these terms? At least partly because the response within the labour movement to unemployment and the unemployed has dealt almost entirely with the first aspect and embarrassingly little with the second. It is the 'regeneration of industry' arguments which predominate, in whatever form or variant of the Alternative Economic Strategy. Here the resolution of the problem of unemployment is posed through the creation of jobs through an expansion of the economy. So, in this spirit, the TUC and the Labour Party have well-produced and increasingly sophisticated publications and proposals on how the economy should be run. Motions on these issues abound at union conferences. But where are the high profile campaigns on welfare rights and benefits, the amount of money the unemployed get, and the way these provisions have been eroded? For the most part, they are absent.

Some might feel this is too harsh. Perhaps. But the tendency within the labour movement to deal with the 'serious' issues of unemployment through the promotion of the Alternative Economic Strategy and to relegate the immediate needs of the unemployed to social policy is there to see if you want to look. For instance, in the Midlands we have had three 'People's Marches' for jobs in three years: national marches in 1981 and 1983 and a Midlands march in 1982. Despite press coverage, all have been successful in terms of giving a continuing publicity to the issue of unemployment and have generated discussion within and support from the *organised* labour movement. But perhaps that says something about the character of the campaign: that the People's March has gained rather more support from people who are employed protesting about their fears and abhorrence of unemployment than from the unemployed themselves.

For instance, how well supported was the 1983 March by the unemployed? Point one: one of the unions that has done most for unemployed members in the Midlands is ASTMS. They have a structure enabling unemployed members to come together, a full-time officer to assist and financial and administrative resources for expenses and education courses. The People's March received extensive support from ASTMS members in the Midlands in the finance and the organising of the March. Yet a meeting of ASTMS unemployed members failed to produce one volunteer to be a marcher. Point two: a group of unemployed people forming an education course in Coventry on issues about unemployment met to discuss their priorities in the demands they would want to make as unemployed and the campaigns they wanted to see develop. 'Marching for Jobs' didn't figure in their list.

These indications of the absence of support from the unemployed for the People's March are scarcely conclusive, but they do suggest that 'passivity' — the-can't-get-the-unemployed-to-do-anything — arguments are insufficient explanations. These were groups of unemployed who were active and wanting to be involved in the issues of unemployment.

Explanations may lie in different directions. Marches themselves discriminate against the involvement of the very young, the aged, disabled or infirm and those with domestic responsibilities; how the March was organised may also have played a part, through the restrictions placed on the activities of the marchers themselves and the sometimes strained relationships between the central organisers and local activists.

But while all these features may be relevant in identifying the undoubted reasons as to why the People's March failed to capture the imagination of the unemployed, perhaps there is something more fundamental. Who, after all, wants to fight for a boring, dirty, soul destroying job? Why should unemployed women want to fight unambiguously for the menial, low-paid jobs they are allocated in our society? Why should former factory workers fight for jobs on the production line? In other words, isn't the kind of work people do and the conditions under which they do it important? 'Production for need' has undoubted qualities as a slogan, but what about the way that production is achieved? These are vital questions that tend to be put to one side and with them the whole issue of socially useful labour in relation to socially useful production.

Popular Planning

Presumably the argument runs that we must get the jobs first and then worry about the conditions and the kind of jobs afterwards.[1] Such a demand is mainly an attempt to return to the previous position of 'full' employment; consequently, it is not surprising that the unemployed are not unambiguously in favour of it. At the same time, the emphasis on jobs clearly indicates why support does flow from the existing workers. Their jobs are in danger.

In many ways the notions of socially-useful production and popular planning derive from the same sources as the radical Alternative Economic Strategy. Heavily connected to notions of industrial regeneration, conventional views of popular planning emanating from the Greater London Council see the importance of socially useful production largely in terms of alternatives to redundancy. The GLC argument for 'Popular Planning' is contained in *Jobs for a Change* (GLC, 1983):

> 'Popular Planning challenges the power of those at the top. It challenges the monopoly which management, politicians and experts have had over co-ordinating and determining economic decisions.

Popular Planning is about so called 'ordinary' people spelling out their vision of the future and fighting to get it implemented.

What is more they are the people who *depend* on jobs in London for their livelihood. These are the people who, if they had the power, would be able to formulate the plans for reconstructing London.

Throughout the pamphlet there are examples of this: the workers at Third Sector, at Austinsuite, at Poco of Romford; the tenants and direct labour workers in Islington; the campaign around the Charlton Skill Centre in Greenwich. There are other examples too, like the workers at Staffa Engineering who occupied their factory to save their jobs and the trade unionists and young people who marched from all parts of London on the People's March for Jobs'. (p.61.)

Predominant in these examples are struggles around job losses and these are identified as very specific moments — when closures/redundancies are imminent or have just been announced. Apart from that, the unemployed — as unemployed — are absent from these examples save for the 'young people' on the People's March. Welfare Rights work and campaigns are not mentioned which presumably means they don't exist or they're not thought sufficiently important to merit a mention.

In reality, the unemployed are usually offered the help of the local Alternative Economic Strategy largely by existing firms — or by co-operatives.[2] It is worth noting that co-operatives themselves, as a modern movement, derived from an era of factory closures and occupations, e.g. Fakenham, Fisher-Bendix, SDN, and Meriden, combined with a relatively radical Department of Trade and Industry when Tony Benn was at the height of his ministerial power. Hilary Wainwright indicates this tradition in spelling out the role of co-operatives quite clearly:

'... our first commitment is to support workers' resistance to closure and redundancy. Co-operatives have serious limitations which no amount of GLC support can overcome.

... co-operatives must be seen not as a permanent solution to the problem of closure and redundancy but as another form of defensive and transitional action'.[3]

Within this framework, co-operatives are tied to existing groups of workers based around the workplace as a point of contact. In some areas this fire-fighting approach has now shifted, with the establishment of local Co-operative Development Agencies (CDAs) who can respond to new groups of people, perhaps unemployed, who want to start co-operatives from scratch. Clearly, this offers the unemployed more choices, yet scarcely other than on a token scale. Whatever the merits of the new co-operatives movement, they can never be, in themselves, the answer to mass unemployment — nor would the

CDAs themselves suggest this might be the case.

So what might be the way in which the clearly desirable arguments for production for social need can be linked to the unemployed? In part this means pressing demands on organisations that can deliver the goods; and for the unemployed, as consumers, this means perhaps the provider of services — housing, health, education, and so on — the local or national state. In that way, genuine local involvement in identifying and planning services is an aspect of socially-useful production where the unemployed can be involved as much as anyone else. Yet in trying to secure resources the unemployed have other problems; it is in this area where we can report on some of the practical work in which we are involved.

Workplace Unions and the Unemployed

Our starting point is that the fight against unemployment does start in the workplace but that the demands of the unemployed also need to be supported by organised labour. That means establishing effective links between the employed and the unemployed. But how?

In the most simple terms, we looked at the workplaces in Coventry where the struggles against redundancy had proved the most effective and tried to identify why the unions there had gained support from their members. Obviously, a complex issue, but the choice of workplace was not difficult. The workplace chosen has a strong trade union organisation with a closed shop and is organised at a sectional/departmental level by elected shop stewards. A Joint Shop Stewards Committee (JSSC) meets weekly and is the main policy making body in the factory. The members have a history of taking firm action to defend agreements and jobs, characterised by a factory occupation in 1982 which achieved the withdrawal of compulsory redundancy notices. Furthermore they have a tradition of assisting those in need, highlighted by support for the unemployed on People's Marches and locally by workplace collections to assist the unemployed with costs associated with attending courses.

One aspect of the JSSC struggles which seemed of particular importance concerned the way that the stewards had kept their members informed of what it was like to be unemployed through regular information on welfare rights. In fact, a welfare rights committee was formed by the stewards to do just that. Our discussions with the stewards have been concerned with how to sustain and develop that initiative. After all, many employed people regularly claim some form of benefit or rebate and this seemed a useful service for the JSSC to maintain and not just reserve for disputes. What is more, an 'educated' membership would have less illusions about what life was like on the dole and hopefully this would establish an inherent resistance to redundancies. But working with the JSSC, it soon became clear that a further development was possible — to ensure:

> '... that as trade unionists that everything possible is done for those that are unemployed trade union members or are unemployed, but live in the community in which we earn our living'. (Welfare Rights/Claimants Committee Proposal.)

Consequently, in conjunction with representatives from the JSSC, we identified three stages in the establishment of a welfare rights/claimants committee: first, the setting up of an effective committee to provide a service for union members in the plant and information on changes to state benefits; second, to expand this service to include unemployed/retired ex-members; third, to provide a service for unemployed members in the community. This reflected the importance of developing an approach which could be expected to be sustained — and the realities of the problem involved, notably the priorities of the JSSC and the attitude of the company.

At this point we are at the first stage, which has involved setting up the structure and responding to the demands of the JSSC. In this area the stewards, with some past experience of using welfare rights committees and a keen awareness of the effectiveness of their own organisation, have clearly identified their priorities and the appropriate organisational structure. These involve certain principles: first, the connection and accountability of the welfare rights committee to the JSSC; second, the representative structure of the committee, based on workgroup and workplace units; third, identification of appropriate sources of materials and ensuring these are available to the committee, as well as keeping them up-to-date; fourth the provision of regular briefings on welfare rights to committee members, who are responsible for relaying information amongst the members they represent.

Our involvement has been particularly with the third and fourth items and in the development of briefing sessions to enable the co-ordinator of the committee to undertake educational work with the committee. The idea here was to develop from an initial programme of sessions around work and benefits to one concerned with the position of the unemployed. Consequently, the initial phase concerns first the needs of the committee in being able to service the requirements of members who are at work, but may be entitled to state benefits because of low income, short-time working or because they are engaged in an industrial dispute. Second, we devise an educational programme that is more geared to meeting the requirements of those without work. While throughout, there is a need to ensure that committee members get a feel for what is going on with the welfare system and the erosions that are taking place.

The demands placed on us were to develop a programme for the briefing sessions, including the necessary teaching materials, for the Committee Co-ordinator to use (he had attended a lay tutor's briefing run by his union, the TGWU). Our response was to produce a two stage course, where many sessions could be run by the co-ordinator, but where some would need the expertise of outside agencies. At this moment the first stage is under way. The progress of this new development is, like similar ones, fairly slow. It is innovative, and makes fresh and unusual demands on people who are already overcommitted as stewards or specialist advice agencies. Nevertheless, we have tried to illustrate two points.

The first simply concerns the method of working, which is consciously to avoid substituting ourselves for the stewards, and to encourage a self-sustaining process not dependent on ourselves as an agency. Second, this work does have every chance of developing links between the unemployed and the employed, not through union hierarchies or abstract plans, but through links between workplaces and local communities. It would indeed be hard to see how an 'alternative product' approach would really assist in the same way. It would certainly be difficult to argue with workers about producing something more socially useful than an agricultural tractor (better tractors maybe, but that is a different issue) and even harder to see why the local community should really care.

What we are really arguing is that we need to think a little more critically about socially useful production, 'alternative products' and 'popular planning' and how these apply to the unemployed. Perhaps 'popular planning' of state benefits should be on the agenda. Does that sound absurd? You might ask yourself why.

The views expressed are those of the authors and do not necessarily reflect either the official views of the Project on which we work or of Coventry Trades Council.

References

1. This it must be stressed has nothing to do with a socialist perspective, since the nature of the struggle and demands made themselves determine the nature of the outcome.

2. An unusual case here is the Bitteswell Employment Alliance which has derived from a factory closure, and where a surprisingly large number of those made redundant have formed themselves into an 'Alliance' in an attempt to develop job opportunities. The question is how general this kind of experience might become, since it is somewhat dependent on the particular skills of those involved and there are a number of resource agencies who are available to provide assistance as and when required.
3. *Socialist Review*, 57, October 1983, p.17.

PATTERNS OF WOMEN'S WORK

1. Most working class women have always *had* to work for money. Prior to the modern industrial period women mainly worked at home producing a wide variety of domestic goods and services of use both to the household and the local community. Industrialisation and the growing conurbations brought about fundamental changes.

2. During the industrial revolution and into the C20th much traditional domestic work was mechanised or rationalised into factory or office systems, or both, often to become *men's* work in large industries. Women's work, then, moved out of the home — split into its unpaid and paid versions. Their jobs mirrored domestic roles as cooks, nurses, secretaries, dressmakers. Advantages were gained though participation in the outside world, with some measure of financial independence.

3. The recession, cuts in public services, new technologies and reactionary appeals to women in their role as carers are eroding women's rightful place in paid productive activity, eroding the gains they have made this century. Women are being pushed back into a 'Victorian' mould of housewife and mother and into new forms of homework made possible by computer equipment, or if they are eligible, by social security.

CHAPTER FIFTEEN
Women Factory Workers — What Could Socially Useful Production Mean for Them?
Sonia Liff

The Chapter by Ursula Huws in this collection describes the transformation, in the post-war period of Britain, of domestic labour processes, together with the restructuring of consumption patterns around a range of factory-produced goods aimed at individual households. These include processed food, clothing and a whole range of domestic appliances. Thus there have been relatively recent and dramatic changes in the way needs have been satisfied both in terms of products and processes. My concern in this Chapter is with food and the food industries.

Discontent over the availability of food, its quality and the conditions under which it has been produced have been important foci of political activity at various times and places. However, socialist analyses of both the current system of food production and possible alternatives have remained underdeveloped. The issues raised are enormous and include the distortion of national economies to provide cash crops; the influence of multinationals over the production, pricing and distribution of foodstuffs; the health of workers and consumers and the connections between methods of farming, processing and marketing.[1]

These broad issues are the backdrop to this Chapter, but its central concern is with women currently working in food processing factories in Britain. The Chapter is not primarily concerned with the way major changes in the location or methods of farming, processing and marketing would affect these women. It is trying to understand the choices these women make as producers and consumers, and within this context to examine some of the possibilities for change.

I am focusing the discussion in this way because I want to draw attention to our failure to take seriously the choices people make in their consumption of food. All too often we are simply scathing about processed food, and romantic about the diet of previous generations, without attempting to undestand why people choose to spend their time and money the way they do. Without such an understanding, socialist alternatives around food are likely to command as little support or interest as 'health foods' or vegetarianism now do, among the majority of working people.

Women in Food Industries

One interesting thing to note about the move to more highly processed food is that women, who have consistently been the main providers of food in the home, also comprise the majority of the workforce in food factories. While this relationship between the work women do in the home and their waged work is often cited to explain occupational sex-typing, I mention it here for rather different reasons. Women are making a choice (albeit a highly structured one) to engage in waged work and to purchase products rather than to concentrate their effort in domestic labour processes. This relationship works both ways in that the availability of such products is a major factor in making it possible for women to combine waged and domestic work.

Why do women make this choice? One thing we can be clear about is that it has very little to do with 'convenience'. Below, two women employed in the food processing industry relate a typical working day.[2] Their descriptions make nonsense of conventional distinctions between production and consumption; home and work; work and leisure.

> 'Say about ten to eight in the morning I'm just getting the breakfast ready for the children, trying to get them up — it takes about half an hour to wake my son up — I'm getting breakfast. I'm just about ready to take my little girl to school she starts about five to nine. Takes about a 15 minute walk — so you can say it's about quarter past nine by the time I get back. Then I'm doing my housework — trying to fit in as much as I can, I'll do the shopping if I need shopping that day. Then I come here for work ... Then I'm coming out again trying to get the tea ready. My son comes home himself, he's home for about half past four and I'm home for about twenty past five. My nephew goes to the same school as my daughter so he takes her to my mother's and I pick her up on the way home. Say about half past six before we sit down for our tea, depends really. Deborah goes to bed about eight. Mark — if I can — I'm usually shouting him from about half past nine to quarter past ten to get to bed. So, you know, you're just trying to fit things in between. Then I'm ready for bed myself'. (A divorced woman with two children working in a meat products factory 1.15-5.15 daily.)

'I go from here, you know, the children have had their breakfast, because me husband gets them off to school and then I start cleaning up, doing my washing and then I go to the shop and then I sit down and have a coffee and then I get my little girl's dinner ready for her coming home from school. She comes home at five past twelve and she goes back about ten past one and I go to bed and she wakes me up at quarter to four and I get up then and make the tea. And then we get tea over for about twenty past six and then I sit and watch the television until I come to work at ten to nine'. (This married woman with four children was working on a *night* shift at a biscuit factory from 9.30pm-7.00am Monday to Thursday. The two and a half hour rest in the afternoon was therefore the only sleep she had during the week.)

Both these women's lives — and those of most of the women in both factories — were highly structured (primarily around their children's needs) and exemplify the difficulties of combining employment with domestic responsibilities. Going out to work at all involves a complex web of arrangements for childcare and the compression of domestic work into almost every available moment.

Nor could one say that there was anything particularly satisfying about the work they were doing. One woman in the biscuit factory described some of the jobs as follows:

'I feel better when I'm not feeding in, to be honest when I'm feeding in I ache all over, you know. It's very nerve racking you've got to keep those shoots filled up . . . Now I don't even mind making boxes because while I'm making boxes I can chat to the girl in front so I don't notice the time going as much. When I'm feeding in . . . the noise of that machine you just can't hear yourself talk so there's no point in chattering, is there? You just plod on like a machine'.

Nevertheless, many of these women had a high commitment to going out to work. Women in the meat products factory were given a questionnaire which included the question:

'Given yourself and your talents and ignoring money, if you were free to get any type of job would you:
a) Want the same kind of work you have now?
b) Prefer to do some other kind of work?
c) Prefer to be a full-time housewife?'

Nearly 400 women completed the questionnaire and of these two-thirds said that they would want to continue working outside the home in these circumstances. However less than 10 per cent of the women said that they would want the same kind of job as they had now. The things women said they liked and disliked about employment reinforced this distinction between work in general and the particular job they were doing. Contact with other women and wages — both for the degree of financial autonomy they provided and for the improvement in living standards they allowed — were spoken of positively; whereas dislikes tended to centre on the job and the factory.

Waged work is seen as desirable, therefore, both for a level of social interaction with other women and for the living standards it allows (at least for two-wage families). Neither of these features are necessary distinctions between domestic and waged work. Absence from waged work does not necessarily imply social isolation and certainly doesn't in many societies. However, the current domestic division of labour, design of housing and lack of community facilities mean that it is the case for most British housewives.

Similarly, the balance between the standard of living that can be achieved with a second wage, (as opposed to more intensive domestic labour), has changed dramatically over time — as have notions of what constitutes a good standard of living. For some goods which are now considered necessities, such as cookers and refrigerators, there is no alternative form of domestic production. For other goods the balance relates to the structure of the market for processed and unprocessed goods. For example, while it is still possible to make one's own clothes it rarely makes sense (in price terms) to do so, even if the most minimal value is given to the producer's time. The establishment of mass markets for processed goods allows them to be cheapened in real terms, thus tipping the balance in their favour.

Many meals can still be made more cheaply from basic food-stuffs than from processed or semi-processed items. Here choices may be more related to the time, skills and resources available to domestic workers. For example, many people wouldn't know how to make, from basic ingredients, things that they routinely eat, (I'm not just thinking of things like curry — what about baked beans?). How many working people find time to make bread? And how many of us would be happy to only eat those fruits and vegetables that were in season?

We also have to accept that our taste in food is very deepseated. Those of us who have grown up on the flavours and textures of processed food find it very difficult to change even when we can see good reasons for doing so — think of the trouble people have reducing the amount of sugar in their diet. Similarly, our class and ethnic background has a strong influence on the foods we eat. As a somewhat perverse consequence, certain foods can become desirable as a way of escaping these definitions: look at the way adverts for instant 'foreign' meals associate these with a whole range of other supposed middle-class practices such as candle-lit dinners. To take a broader example, a child in home-made clothes is more likely to feel this reflects the poverty rather than the skill of her/his mother.

Women in Waged Work and Socially Useful Production

Having looked at some of the reasons why women go out to work and choose to buy certain products and at a few of the factors which structure these choices, we can ask 'What type of policy concerned with socially useful production would be relevant to these women?' This question is particularly critical at a time when increasing automation is destroying many women's jobs within factories, and cuts in social services and persistent male unemployment are resulting in pressure on women to give up waged work.

Firstly, it is important to endorse analyses which call for a widening of debates around the Alternative Economic Strategy and Workers' Plans. Feminist critics have argued that alternatives must be refocused to address childcare and broader aspects of domestic work. Important as this is, it should not prevent us from thinking about a whole range of other issues relating to the goods women produce and the way they produce them. We need to think about the specific problems and opportunities presented by women's jobs; about the product of their work and their position as waged and unpaid domestic workers, in comparison with the groups of men who have been the more usual focus of discussions about socially useful production.

Returning to a consideration of foodstuffs, one alternative frequently proposed is a return to less processed food. While this can be justified on the basis of price and improved diet, and should certainly form part of a strategy, the foregoing discussion suggests many reasons why it would not, on its own, be a very popular alternative. In addition, a contraction in food processing would have severe implications for women's job opportunities in manufacturing, for, unlike most engineering machines, the equipment within food processing factories is highly 'dedicated' — that is specifically designed to do particular jobs. Thus, the chances of finding alternative *products* are minimal, and to keep the support of women workers we would need to couple this strategy with one that explicitly aimed to break down occupational sex-typing and open up more jobs to women. This is not just a matter of including women within some 'grand plan', but of seeing that alternatives cannot be constructed at the level of one food factory or even at that of the entire industry.

Given that a return to less processed food would imply an increase in domestic labour we also need to extend our analysis to consider the way this is divided. In the current situation any extra work would fall largely on women and our strategy would ignore the needs of those women who want to, or have to, go out to work (or those who simply don't want to spend a large proportion of their time in the kitchen). Without even considering what people like to eat we can, therefore, see many reasons why an alternative strategy for food must address the issue of processed food both in terms of its quality and in terms of the work needed to produce it.

One way of starting to do this would be to find positive ways of using women's dual roles as producers and consumers of processed food. These aspects of food production have generally been kept very separate. Market researchers test new products on shoppers, who may also be workers in food factories; but as employees women have never been encouraged to become involved in changing the type of things produced.

Managers, however, have recognised a potential use to them in this link between domestic and waged workers. In both factories mentioned above, appeals were often made to women's domestic roles in an attempt to get them to keep the area in which they worked clean and tidy. This is explicitly described as 'housekeeping' and is usually adhered to if only because to do otherwise results in a work area which is both unpleasant and dangerous.

Other attempts by management could potentially back-fire. In the meat products factory there were signs saying 'If you wouldn't buy it, don't pack it'. This was an attempt to introduce some quality control into the packing process. The women I spoke to said that if they were to take this seriously they would be doing very little packing! An individual woman trying to improve quality in this way would be unlikely to remain in employment long, but if all the women packers acted together and publicised their activities the effects could be dramatic.

Similarly, food workers often have information about products which could be useful to consumers. For example, the biscuit factory directed identical biscuits onto two packing lines. One wrapped them into cheap supermarket 'own brand' packages the other under a higher price 'quality' label. If examples like this could be made more widely known it could help expose the reality behind the apparently wide variety of products on offer and allow shoppers to choose on the basis of the product not the package.

There would be problems with such strategies if they were adopted only by women in one factory. In such a case they could result in merely damaging one firm's position against its competitors. This would adversely affect the employment opportunities of its workers and would be unlikely to have any lasting affect on the quality of food. To be successful such strategies must be organised by broadly based groupings of producers and consumers. There are few existing bodies on which to base such a development. However, since most women live very close to where they work, we might encourage tenants groups and trade union branches to develop links for such purposes. Initiatives of this kind may seem a long way off, but the work of various trade union research and resource centres, such as MERG at Manchester,[3] has already shown the necessity for workers to have closer links (both between different factories and between unions) in order to respond effectively to change.

The forging of new links could also help to make consumer action — such as boycotts — more effective. For example, while many of us still won't buy food from South Africa it is very difficult, as an individual examining labels in the supermarket, to feel that it makes any difference. If such activities could be carried out in a more collective and integrated way, (for example picketing shops which sell certain items, preferably with the workers involved) they would have a much greater impact. Retailers are quite willing to promote themselves as providers of what they believe their customers as a group want — take Marks and Spencer's stress on the proportion of British made goods in their stores — so there is reason to believe they would be susceptible to this type of pressure.

It is difficult for women to intervene in redirecting the production process. Most women food workers are employed in the packing area on extremely repetitive operations. This work gives little access to, or knowledge about, the production process. Few women's education or experience has equipped them with the scientific or technical skills necessary to make a direct intervention into the redesign of products or processes. Most women in the food industry are unionised, but few take an active role in union activities. Whilst this is partly a problem of women's domestic commitments (and this particularly applies to part-time workers) it is also a response to the amount of interest many women feel the unions have in them.[4]

Women Workers, Male Workers: Problems, Strategies

All this underlines the differences between the position of women factory workers and male craft workers. Strategies appropriate for male engineering workers, with a wide range of skills and access to research and development work, begin to look rather hollow in this context. Workers' Plans developed by democratically based groups drawn from all groups in the factory and from the wider community could theoretically improve this situation. However, these would probably still give women a marginal and indirect influence on developments. We need to recognise that there are real differences of interest and power between groups of workers which will not be overcome simply by a process of 'getting everyone together'. All groups need to have ways of assessing, and if necessary challenging, the plans that are being put forward.

These are critical problems that we cannot afford to ignore. For it is at this level that groups of workers could develop plans for socially useful production directed at, among other things, improving the nutritional value of foods, reducing additives, improving production processes and the quality of jobs. If women do not have a voice in these discussions it is likely that their needs and interests will be overlooked.

There is no instant solution, but better education and training could certainly make a difference. Unions should insist that all workers are given an understanding of the entire production process not just of the little bit on which they are to work. Similarly, they should press management to allow day-release for workers to go on any course which is relevant to the work of the firm, not just to their own job. Local authorities should support centres which are being set up to encourage women to undertake non-traditional training, and should re-examine the recruitment and teaching practices of courses they currently support. We might also wish to press for changes in what is taught in schools under the label of 'domestic science', or maybe even abolish it altogether in favour of a broader based subject.

Unions, and other organisations, need to examine the ways they conduct their activities to see how these might discourage women from participation. And women need to develop the skills to force them to change! However, none of these suggestions can really remove the need for women to have jobs which give them a broader experience of the production process and from which they can influence developments. Unions could start by pushing for job rotation agreements which crossed traditional job boundaries (particularly between 'men's jobs' and 'women's jobs'). From this beginning it might be possible to work towards a 'reintegration' of tasks, so that all jobs contain more variety and discretion. In the longer term, the degree to which groups of workers can progressively restructure the division of labour will perhaps serve as a test of whether movements for socially useful production can break out of their engineering origins and become relevant to the majority of workers in manufacturing.

References

1. A very readable introduction to the issues is *More than We Can Chew*, Charlie Clutterbuck and Tim Lang, Pluto Press, 1982.
2. The research described was carried out as part of a project called 'Pressures on Women Engaged in Production Line Work' which was funded by the Medical Research Council and the Department of Employment.
3. MERG can be contacted at 202, Oxford Road, Manchester. There is a paper on their work with workers at Kellogs and Smith Crisps called 'Chips and Crisps. The Impact of New Technology on Food Processing Jobs in Greater Manchester' by Bernard Leach and John Shutt.
4. The role of women within trade unions is discussed in *Hear This Brother — Women Workers and Union Power* by Anna Coote and Peter Kellner, *New Statesman*, 1980 and in *Getting it Together* by Jenny Beale, Pluto Press, 1982.

CHAPTER SIXTEEN
Alternative Products in West Berlin: Mehringhof, Netzwerk and Goldrausch
Erica Carter

In Great Britain, economic alternatives to the ravages of Thatcherism are most commonly conceived in terms of corporate planning. The outline of Labour's alternative economic strategy (AES), published in October 1980 by the London working group of the Conference of Socialist Economists (CSE), argues that economic decline should be combated first through State intervention and control.[1]

This encompasses reflation of the economy through increases in public spending, together with planned controls on foreign trade and the movements of international capital; an industrial strategy of extended public ownership; and a national economic plan to co-ordinate macroeconomic policies with industrial planning and price control. Second, the process of reconstruction will take place on the level of a 'network of industrial democracy' which, it is claimed, will eventually 'introduce widespread democratisation and substitute social for market forms of control'.[2] Throughout the CSE document, the AES is viewed as an indispensable framework for direct action: without such a corporate plan democratic initiatives which work from the bottom up are seen to remain both marginal and ineffective.

Within what has become known as West Germany's 'alternative economy' we encounter a very different order of economic and political priorities. In the first instance, the difference is one of temporal perspective. Since the Thatcher Government was returned to power in June 1983, hopes for the success of a British alternative economic strategy have had to be deferred to a projected — but uncertain — future with a Labour government in power. In West Germany on the other hand, political developments since the early 1970s have fostered the growth of a heterogeneous 'alternative movement', incorporating strands from anarchism, feminism, citizen's action groups, ethnic minority politics and the post-Maoist Left. Linking these diverse political groups is a common emphasis on the 'here and now' of political alternatives, on partial and small-scale transformations in the present as a necessary means to desired future ends. In terms of economic strategy, this has meant experimenting with economic forms which occupy a space *between* the State and the market, operating in continuous tension with both of these.

I shall describe models of such experimentation with alternative economic form based in West Berlin, firstly the Mehringhof, a collectively administered factory and workshop complex. Then we shall look at two alternative finance networks both of which are tenant organisations in the Mehringhof — Netzwerk and Goldrausch.

Mehringhof

Mehringhof, consisting of two five-storey factory and workshop blocks, is sited in the working class district of Kreuzberg Berlin and is collectively run. Since the Mehringhof idea was floated in 1977, its founding members had a struggle in the first instance to find and then to purhcase the building. Formed as a limited company, in order to secure grants and loans, the members worked out a model whereby ownership could pass gradually out of the hands of the company and into those of the tenants, with the tenants' association taking over progressively more shares. The intention then being to neutralise capital and at the same time to collectivise the property.

In its introductory brochure Mehringhof is described as 'primarily a common roof for projects which work independently of each other in their own particular areas'. This is in contrast to unified production co-operatives such as the Ufa-Gelände in Berlin Tempelhof, which provides both living and working space for an enclosed relatively self-sufficient community. Each project in Mehringhof is represented on a central steering committee, whose duties range from organising cleaning rotas for the central courtyard, to financing repairs and deciding on the admission of new projects to the collective. Groups applying to move into Mehringhof must fulfil a range of criteria, including collective administration, profit sharing, a degree of independence from the state, the church or other institutions, and agreement to participate in steering committee duties.

Thus, for a sketch of the mechanics of the Mehringhof collective; what then of the wider implications of this and similar projects? As far as its organisational forms are concerned, there are dissenting voices within Mehringhof itself: the building houses an 'Initiative for the sale of Mehringhof', which defines itself as 'opposed in principle to private ownership of land and housing', and criticizes Mehringhof for allowing the day-to-day teething troubles of the alternative economy to deflect its attention away from more pressing political issues in the 'outside world'. From a British perspective, however, there is little to be gained by attempting to unravel the intricacies of these internal tensions; more can be learned by reconstructing the relations within which Mehringhof gains significance as a political project.

In the present framework — a handbook of socially useful *production* — this work of contextualisation is particularly important; for, as a glance at the list of its member projects shows, Mehringhof has become a focal point for collective initiatives in the *marketing* and *distribution* of goods and services (with a bias towards 'cultural commodities' — books, magazines, alternative arts and leisure), but seems at first sight largely to have neglected the spheres of primary and secondary production. (The projects are listed at the end of this Chapter.) An exception to this rule is the engineering collective Wuseltronick, which has been involved in research and development projects for wind power stations. In this respect, the Mehringhof collective is typical of the estimated 11,500 alternative projects in West Germany and West Berlin, 70 per cent of which operate in the 'tertiary' or 'service' sector — transport and distribution services; leisure, information and public relations; administration and welfare services.

It would, however, be misleading to equate the tertiary sector of the 'regular' or 'formal' economy with the alternative projects described here. In capitalist enterprises, economic activity is geared to the drive for capital accumulation. The alternative movement, on the other hand, shows some affinity with early Utopian socialism in its attempt to dethrone exchange value from the centre of the economic stage, and to restore categories of use value and production for social need.

In this context, 'productive' labour is seen not only as that labour which produces commodities for market exchange — a definition derived from Marx — but also as the labour through which social relations, cultural meanings and values are, equally, 'produced'. Economic exchange in this scale of priorities is subordinated to new forms of social exchange, to friendship and communality at sites of 'work' and 'leisure'. Thus profits — such as they are — are channelled into financial aid for other collectives, or forfeited to the 'alternative community' to which these projects belong. What this means in practice can best be illustrated by a campaign conducted by Ökotopia, a retailing and publishing co-operative in Mehringhof, whose range of goods includes Nicaraguan coffee, wine from various European production collectives, and tea imported from India and elsewhere. In 1982, Ökotopia began a tea campaign which aimed to raise the share of third world producers in profits from retailing in first world countries.[3]

Ökotopia, like other initiatives in alternative marketing, depends for its survival on the support of what mainstream marketing would identify as a specific 'market segment': consumers whose sympathies with oppressed groups — in this case, third world producers — are expressed amongst other things in terms of alternative tastes and 'lifestyles'. Ökotopia's customers are prepared to go out of their way (literally and metaphorically) to travel to Mehringhof to buy tea, coffee, wine or bread; more than price, it is political sympathies which determine consumer choice on this alternative market.

Just how precarious this makes the situation of some autonomous projects is manifest in the present difficulties of women's bookshops in West Berlin. Founded on the crest of the first wave of seventies feminism, women's bookshops began to flounder when other Left and commercial bookshops expanded their own feminist sections to meet growing demand for books by, for and about women. Even the firmest of feminist convictions faltered when books previously found only in women-only bookshops in far-flung corners of the city became readily available on local bookstalls. But it is not only competition of this kind which threatens the survival of alternative and feminist enterprises; geared as they are primarily towards the production of social use values (as opposed to the profit motive), they suffer chronic financial instability. In pursuit of autonomy and self-determination at the workplace, project members must in practice be prepared to invest months or years of unpaid labour into a venture which, in most cases, is unlikely to become financially viable without injections of capital from the State or other sources. They face, then, two routes to financial stability: accumulating capital through long periods of unpaid labour, and grants or loans from outside bodies. It is this second area which I want to consider by looking at alternative finance networks in West Berlin.

Networking: Goldrausch and Netzwerk

There are at present two autonomous finance networks based in West Berlin and operating from Mehringhof. Goldrausch, the more recent of the two, is a feminist network which was launched in 1983 following struggles between Netzwerk and sections of the women's movement over the former's allocation of funds. As in Great Britain, the women's movement in West Germany, hitherto reliant on State funding for many of its activities, now finds itself fighting over a shrinking slice of the government's financial cake. Funding alternatives are in desperate demand; but Goldrausch is still in its infancy, and it is too early to make any assessment of its long-term prospects. In terms of its internal 'mechanics' however, Goldrausch takes Netzwerk as its model; it may therefore be most helpful to begin by sketching in some of the details of the Netzwerk system.

Netzwerk Selbsthilfe (Self-help Network) is not only one of the oldest and most firmly established projects in Mehringhof; more than this, as a funding body which strives to maintain independence both from the State and from Capital, it functions as a linchpin in the alternative infrastructure of West Berlin and the Federal Republic. Founded in West Berlin in 1978, it aimed to 'make political action at once less terrifying and less defensive' by offering financial and organisational assistance to collective projects and political initiatives within the city. By 1980, thirty independent Netzwerk centres had been set up across West Germany; the West Berlin project remained the largest of all, with a total of 3,000 members (as against a Netzwerk membership of 3,000 in the rest of the country).

Netzwerk operates on the basis of small but regular monthly subscriptions from individual members or groups, together with the occasional 'one-off' donation. The recommended subscription is one per cent of net monthly income, or DM10 (approximately £2.50) for students, school students and the unemployed. The money flows into a central fund, to be redistributed in the form of grants or loans (the latter are preferred) to projects which meet specific criteria for Netzwerk aid. Projects applying for financial assistance must produce evidence of their 'broadly social, educative and/or emancipatory character', identified by such criteria as collective organisation, profit-sharing, and readiness to collaborate with other 'alternative' projects. Other more 'pragmatic' requirements include stability of membership within the collective, and a long-term perspective of financial independence; exceptions to this second contention are projects in education, community action, and the arts, or political campaigns.

Decisions on the allocation of funds are taken by an advisory committee which comprises twenty members: eight delegates from existing collectives, six elected members' representatives and six members chosen by random selection. Once an application for funds has been made, the advisory committee directs applicants to a smaller working party which processes the application and gives advice on the most effective use of grants or loans. Feasibility studies of individual projects are then passed back to the advisory committee, which takes the final decision on the allocation of funds (while remaining bound by members' decisions on the broad nature of projects to be supported). The 'management' of Netzwerk, meanwhile, rests in the hands of a steering committee, elected by the Netzwerk membership for a period of two years, and responsible for technical organisation, administration and public relations.

Indirect State Dependence and Autonomous Fury

Both Netzwerk and Goldrausch understand themselves as autonomous bodies functioning independently of the State, as well as industrial and commercial capital. Yet the notion of autonomy should not be confused with defection to an isolated hinterland of feminist and alternative culture. In economic terms alone, both these finance networks are crucially dependent on indirect government aid, many of the sympathisers on whose incomes they depend being themselves employed by the State. (Josef Huber estimates that State employees make up one quarter of the Netzwerk membership, and that their contributions comprise as much as 60 per cent of its total funds). Similarly, it would be illusory to suppose that autonomous funding could ever represent an absolute alternative to State or commercial aid. Applicants to Netzwerk must produce evidence of previous applications to governmental and other funding bodies — and a recent special issue of the feminist magazine *Courage* on women's self-help projects placed Netzwerk and Goldrausch at the very bottom of a list of possible sources of finance. To quote *Courage*: 'at the latest in the financing stage, it becomes clear that women's projects are by no means free-floating islands, but dependent bodies in the wider structures of the capitalist market'.

Economic dependencies do not always bring subordination, just as islands do not inevitably float free. The Mont St. Michel in Brittany is an island at high tide, a peninsula at low tide: Arctic ice floes connect with the land mass at points, reconstituting themselves to break away later in different shapes and forms. The Netzwerk emblem is known as 'die rasende Sau': 'rasend', an ambiguous epithet meaning furious, frantic ... or raving, demented, mad. 'Goldrausch' (Goldrush) has other connotations too: 'der Rausch' — drunken fit, drunkenness, intoxication ... or delirium, frenzy, transport, ecstasy. There is no fixity in these images: 'networking' at its best involves a constant process of dismantling old dependencies, forging new connections, producing new fields of cultural experience.

In West Berlin, alternative culture moves restlessly *between* the encrusted structures of capitalist enterprise and the welfare state. Self-help projects perform services which the State will not — and in many cases cannot — provide; alternative 'enterprises' produce and distribute goods and services to a section of the Berlin population whose needs are never met by capitalist producers. In recognition of these strengths, the Centre Right of the Christian Democrat Party in government has increasingly abandoned its old 'hard-line' approach to the alternative movement, preferring instead to use self-help initiatives as a means of relieving pressure on State funded social services. It is *minority* cultures of opposition which alternative projects represent and serve; but these projects can no longer be easily dislodged from the economic and cultural niche they have colonised.

PROJECTS IN MEHRINGHOF

Committee of Inquiry (Ermittlungsausshuss) into State harassment of squatters (established December 1980 following police brutality and mass arrests on squatters' demonstrations).
Gesundheitsladen Berlin e.V. (Health information and resource centre).
Netzwerk Selbsthilfe e.V. (Finance network).
Stattwerke (Advice and resource centre for collective and 'alternative' projects).
Stattbuch Verlag GmbH (Publishing co-operative: publications include a guide to alternative projects in West Berlin).
Tax Advisory Service *(Steuerberater)*
Wuseltronick. Engineering collective, involved in research, development and production for wind power stations and industrial electronics. One result of work to date has been the development of an electronic system for the measurement of vibration in moving machine parts.
Graph Druckula (Graphics and printing co-operative).
CaDeWe (Political cabaret troupe).
Verlagsgesellschaft Gesundheit mit beschränkter Haftung (Publishing co-operative: a 'forum and mouthpiece for all groups and individuals concerned with the reorientation of the

dominant system of curative medicine and social welfare').
Lernbörse ('Education Exchange': co-ordinates educational needs with professional skills, by establishing contacts between teachers on the one hand, and students approaching the Lernbörse with specific requirements on the other).
Schule für Erwachsenenbildung (Adult Education (teachers' and students') collective, founded 1973).
Wechselwirkung (Quarterly journal of technology, science and society).
Transit (Publishing co-operative).
Zitronenpresse (Women's publishing co-operative: works in conjunction with *Adele Meyers Herstellungsbüro*, a one-woman production office producing books on contract from other publishers).
Film/video co-op (makes mainly documentary films on 'history-work-everyday life').
Kirschkern (Mail-order books).
Forschungs- und Dokumentationszentrum Chile-Lateinamerika (FDCL) (Chilean and Latin American research and documentation centre).
Latein-Amerika Nachrichten (Latin America News).
Ökotopia (Retailing and publishing co-operative, incorporating a training scheme for apprentices to the retail trade).
Regenbogen Film (Animated film collective).
Theaterei (comprises three theatre projects: *Fliegendes Theater, Hans Wurst Nachrichten* and *Pfifferling*).
Alternative Liste Kreuzberg.
AK Orientierungs- und Bildungshilfe e.V. (Adult literacy project).
Freie Schule Kreuzberg (Kreuzberg Free School).
Fahrradwerkstatt mehringhof (Bicycle workshop).
Freunde der Erde (Friends of the Earth).
Pille Palle und die Ötterpötter (Rock band).
AUSSERHALB (Women's rock band).
Kinderschappen Mehringhof e.V. (Playgroup).
CeBeef (Club for the disabled and friends).
Ambulante Dienste e.V. (Ambulance Service for the disabled).
ATIF/Verein der Arbeiter aus der Türkei (Turkish Workers' Association).
Tu'ng Dojo (Karate, judo and self-defence).
Initiative verkauft den Mehringhof e.V. (Initiative for the sale of Mehringhof: 'We are opposed as a matter of principle to private ownership of land and housing . . . (we see Mehringhof as) the initiator of the problem. On the one hand, radical slogans are thrown around, on the other, we no longer turn up for

demonstrations, because the Senator is coming to visit, or the alternative economy is having teething troubles').
Filmcafe.

Address: Mehringhof, Gneisenaustr.2, 1000 Berlin 61.

References
1. CSE London Working Group. *The Alternative Economic Strategy. A Labour Movement Response to the Economic Crisis.* CSE, London 1980, p.44.
2. *Ibid.*, p.8.
3. *Courage Sonderheft Nr.8. Arbeitsplätze selder schaffen!* Courage 1983, p.67.

FROM PUBLIC OWNERSHIP TO PRIVATE PROFIT

Since 1979 a strategy has been developed by the Thatcher government to deliver an 'enterprise Culture' (the New Right's name for *laissez-faire*). This has produced an array of legislation, the main categories of which we headline below.
- Sale of companies in public ownership by share issue on the Stock Exchange, e.g. British National Oil Corporation and British Telecom.
- Stripping of nationally owned assets by sales to private buyers. Land, machinery, buildings etc have all been disposed of in this way.
- The setting up of joint ventures between the public and private sectors.
- Creating and promoting private competition where previous state monopoly existed.
- The cutting of public provision creating avenues for private companies. This is linked to the encouragement of private contractors in tendering for public sector services — catering, laundry, transport, refuse collection and so on.
- Schemes to introduce private finance into large public construction projects, like road building.

We can see then that a policy towards the public sector is being accomplished through a pincer movement of legislative means, reduction of resources and expenditure cuts. The trickle of different forms of attack on the public sector is turning into a flood. Here are some examples.

COMMUNICATIONS

Telecommunications
- 1981 Postal service and telecommunications split.
- 1982 A 25 year licence granted to Mercury to run independent telecommunication system under new powers granted to Secretary of State for Industry.
- Post Office monopoly suspended for private operators to run certain mail services.
- 1984 British Telecom sold.

ENERGY

Oil
— 1981 British National Oil Corporation converted to limited liability company — Britoil.

Gas/Electricity
— Private sector encouraged to supply greater amount of electricity.
— Proposed sale of gas showrooms which currently provide appliance sales and service, consumer advice, information and payment facilities, and of British Gas itself.

TRANSPORT

Air
— Plans to sell shares in British Airways and dissolve British Airways Board.

Rail
— Subsidiary company set up to handle introduction of private capital into some British Rail operations — sea/hover.
— BR hotels sold on open market.

Road
— Express coach services developed by private operators to compete with National Bus Company, which itself is to be sold.

LOCAL AUTHORITY SERVICES

Privatisation proposals in refuse collection, cleaning, catering, building maintenance, school meals, housing management and local authority auditing.

Social Services
— Government's grants to Local Authorities reduced.
— Followed by rate-capping. Local Authorities heavily penalised for overspending.

Education (primary and secondary)
— Larger classes, increased teacher workloads, fewer teacher training places, pressure on parents to provide 'frills' — school trips, and 'basics' stationery, tuition in cultural subjects like music. Government assisted places scheme to private schools increased. Emphasis on training for work even in secondary schools.

(higher)
— Social sciences attacked, humanities and arts reduced, fewer research awards, staff and departments cut. Authentic knowledge is being redefined as empiricism.

Welfare Services

The Tories are changing the concept of care *in* the community to care *by* the community.

— Provision of day-care facilities, home-help and meals services, residential homes for elderly, young offenders and children in care have all been affected.

— Leaving those in need to be catered for by private operations, overstretched voluntary organisations, or where neighbours and relatives can be called upon, they take up the slack with a reduced scale of support service and finance, often with high personal wear and tear. Mostly women perform this work *for* the rest of the community.

National Health Service

— Hospital and ward closures. Only 10 out of 72 District Health Authorities who responded to the *Guardian* Survey of DHAs have avoided making cuts (18.1.84).

— Staff cuts, consultant posts left vacant, and reduction of appointments of junior doctors (2-3,000 unemployed doctors in 5 health districts estimated in the British Medical Association's Junior Doctors Survey). In September 1983 Norman Fowler announced a reduction of 5,000 in nursing staff levels. This is on top of reduced hours. Private contractors claim they will only employ 3 out of 4 existing ancillary workers.

— Asset-stripping. NHS land 7 per cent of 50,000 acres sold. Staff accommodation worth £1 billion sold.

— Expansion of private medical insurance and private hospital and medical services; continued uncontrolled growth of drug industry which makes huge profits.

— 'We were explicitly instructed by the management not to talk to patients in the firm's time. So that cheering up sick and distressed persons even for a couple of minutes was disapprovingly categorised as wasting time.' Letter to *Guardian* from a health worker 22.2.83.

— Conditions of work and pay worsened, time schedules tightened, lower standards of work reported from some hospitals when assessing the performance of private contractors providing catering, laundry or cleaning services.

In the face of all this and worse to come what is needed — a new dose of nationalisation or new democratic forms of public ownership?

Conclusion

This book has shown, then, that there is no single object, movement or project which completely contains and delimits the term socially useful production.

Although we have seen how Socially Useful Production has developed as a complex idea which spans services, products, labour processes, political demands, political theories and social ideas, we have also borne in mind its relationship to the specific needs, economic, political and cultural of particular people: young, old; black, white; male, female; fit, unfit; skilled, unskilled; oppressed, liberated.

We have also seen the progress from the rise of workers combine committees and observed the displacement of much of their effort into the projects developed by Metropolitan County Councils. While such evolution has taken place in a politically hostile environment, we have recognised the earlier vulnerability of Socially Useful Production, when fixed to a single site and power base, and the progress towards its extension across multiple sites.

What we would stress is that SUP should provide the basis for a strong exuberant politics and practice which can both challenge the logics that capital deploys and sustain the growth of oppositional visions and forms.

Thinking Socially Useful Production

The SUP critique and alternative should not be limited to the commodity side of commodity production. We need, also, to insist on the right of everyone to the opportunity to do meaningful work. This involves asking questions about the products of labour and the techniques and processes by which they are produced. A transfer to socially useful commodities would not in itself guarantee the creation of a socially useful labour process. Nor can this be brought about simply through changes at the workplace, leaving the rest of life untouched. This becomes clear when looking at the domestic work done by women. New household commodities often fail to reduce the scale of household tasks (sometimes they enlarge them!) and, rather than socialising domestic work to include all household members, help to reinforce the women's housekeeping role.

Clearly conditions of work must not be forgotten, since many sections of the workforce have not yet won reasonable conditions. When looking at the problems that most concern working women it is obvious that SUP has to address socially useful and equitable conditions for work as well as products and labour processes. Equal pay may be on the statute books, but is not a reality for many women. Securing maternity/paternity agreements, the provision of adequate childcare, hours of work on a daily and weekly basis, protecting part-time as well as full-time jobs to enable parents to spend time with children are all issues which expand the meaning of social usefulness.

But most centrally, the demand for SUP is a demand that we gain personal and collective power over our own lives. We often think of 'power' as a property of persons — that there are groups who boss, dominate and oppress other groups. While this is visibly true, it has been argued that we need to consider power as accountable to no particular group but flowing through many aspects of life — for example into systems of thought, characteristic modes of behaviour, and bureaucratic organisations. Certainly the current restructuring of capitalism on a world scale *is* concerned with maximising profits, but this is not some neutral economic goal that can be achieved through a set of technical exercises. It can only happen by creating new systems which are designed to limit our autonomy and choice as workers; which abolishes a whole range of human skills, and disciplines us to the demands of complex systems. Production is not only about making goods, it is also about creating workers: persons who are trained so that they possess necessary skills, and also trained in that other sense of disciplined to behave appropriately. Commodity production demands both the cheap availability of our labour power and that our ideas, desires, behaviour and way of life are subordinated to its needs. A major feature of contemporary capitalism is the ability of multinational companies to switch production to many parts of the world in search of vital resources — not only for raw materials, but also for an unsophisticated or well disciplined workforce.

This transnational power of capitalism makes it necessary for SUP, as a political project, also to transcend particular countries. This is given a sharper edge as we know that we are all faced with the possibility of an annihilating nuclear war. Certainly the arms trade is still the central support of most major economies. We have to face up to the task of transforming not individual firms but whole economies from the creation of weapons of terror to socially useful production.

Stated baldly, all this can read like science fiction: some vast conspiracy of people who are trying to undermine our very lives. We all know that the reality is more partial and ragged than this; that it lacks the neat formulation and tidy edges of an account. But we should not lose sight of dominant tendencies or the size of the problem merely because they are difficult to describe in a few lines. To be more specific, we need to recognise that in the struggle to give reality to the ideas of SUP we are trying to unpick some of the major features of the capitalist system of production. Through demanding the right to determine for ourselves what commodities we produce and the conditions and sets of relationships through which they are produced, we also implicitly demand a radical break in the way in which the present processes create us as workers and construct us as persons. While the present system might accommodate (in some cases, welcome and make money out of) design and production of new 'alternative' products, it is clearly not prepared or, indeed, able to renegotiate the whole basis on which we live.

SUP, then, is antithetical to the central logic of capitalism and attempts to re-integrate aspects of life which capitalism has, over the centuries, managed to separate and compartmentalise. One problem in facing so major a task is that for the most part we do not experience 'capitalism' as a system of economic domination and exploitation. Indeed, we rarely think of it at all. We live our lives under capitalism as 'ordinary' life; we live out the logic of capitalism as 'common sense'. Mrs Thatcher's version of what is currently happening to the UK is that a 'new industrial revolution' is in progress; a new organisation of industry is taking place with painful temporary consequences. The inefficient are going to the wall and will be replaced by dynamic new firms provided that we are all prepared to be flexible and not demand high wages or full employment. The Welfare State, once seen as an articulation of collective needs through collective contribution, is now represented as a vast state charity to which, on future projections, only the utterly destitute need apply. The central institution for the satisfaction of needs will be the family and not any family structure but that mythically 'normal' family which has Dad at work, Mum running the home, and the kids at school.

Men are being told that they only have a chance of a job if they are prepared to work for 'realistic' (low) wages and do not disrupt the flow of production through union action. Women are being overtly told that their place is the home and are being disciplined to accept the role of provider to the family and nurse to the sick and aged. However, we should acknowledge that the SUP initiatives of recent years have raised few questions about domestic labour. Indeed they have been concerned with changes in products and labour processes, but not with the transformation of the whole concept of production. Many women have been marginalised within or excluded from the dominant, male version of 'production' and much of the paid and unpaid work they do has been treated as 'supportive' or secondary. If SUP is to be a viable political project, we need to question seriously the ways in which it has made radical demands within existing structures, but left untouched the system of male privilege and dominance which structures our conception of 'work'.

Perhaps just because the SUP movement originated in the engineering and arms industries, and has been an overwhelmingly masculine project, feminists have been loathe to engage with the issues and their presentation. But feminists have certainly been active over issues relating to their own experience: the effects of new technologies on traditional areas of women's work, or the inadequacies of public service provisions to meet women's needs are two examples. In this respect modern feminism has been a separate strand of political concern about social usefulness for women, but with wider salience for all people. The recovery of a lost history of feminist action towards the building of desirable, useful domestic housing and urban centres, and other areas of concern to working, public and private life make it clear that women have been concerned with social usefulness over a long period. (See the box on Utopias.) That said though, it is far from easy for women to be involved with workplace issues, since they are often in semi or unskilled jobs; furthermore unions are not always willing to make female participation possible, let alone to question the products or services they work to make. Only when changes at these sorts of levels are undertaken will the SUP project be of real interest to feminists, and hope to find a place on the agenda of the women's movement.

We should recall that the present condition of our social life is represented to us not as a necessary evil but as a return to older, saner ways of life — to 'Victorian virtues'. Mobilised on its behalf is a notion of Great Britain as an imperialist nation which can regain its power (described as 'self respect') if we all consent to act out the roles prepared for us. Thus we will achieve the best of all worlds: a modernity which transforms work and industry underpinned by 'traditional' values and ways of life.

In response to this we need to be clear what our relationship is to restructuring and to its incorporation and representation by ruling groups. In this respect it is often difficult, but necessary, to avoid a nostalgic yearning to return to the old practices. A desire for the reinstatement of craft skills, for things that last, made with care and yielding satisfaction to the maker. Many of the old crafts were difficult, dangerous and involved workers in long hours of dull toil. Rather than longing for old technologies, values and practices, we need to transfer new technical developments into a creative work process.

The Tories have won two elections and seem to have tapped a vein of popular support and sentiment. SUP initiatives have to work to provide alternative versions of reality, to undermine this ideological terrain, as well as produce alternative products. We have to extend the idea of collective planning and decision making outside the firm or industry to all aspects of our social lives. This means re-inventing and vitalising the ideas that led to the construction of the Welfare State and connecting initiatives into programmes of genuinely popular planning and control.

The Welfare State — Privatised Nightmare of Social Vision?

The public services should be vital attempts to match needs with services and products largely outside the market relations. The corner-stone of belief in public services has been the right of each to decent health and social care, education, housing and safe environmental services regardless of status or the capacity to pay. As employment the public sector upholds the right to useful work — that is social *well*-fare as productive labour, and productive labour as a form of well-being.

The state of the public sector may be seen as part of a larger process involving the national direction of global restructuring, the changing relation between state and capital and the redefinition of the State and responsibilities of active government. The rolling back of the State enables appropriation and intervention by sections of capital and at the same time the parameters of social needs and provisions to meet them are being re-drawn by the reduction of the resource base, cuts, the re-allocation of ownership and control — privatisation, as a practice and as an ideology. We are invited to take shares in the 'ownership' of British Telecom, a nationalised asset belonging to every citizen!

It must be recognised that restructuring is rooted on some fertile soil. The ways people perceive their needs and the ways they are met have shifted. The fusion of need and desire into an endless cornucopia of commodities has helped to devalue the skills, services and care of human labour. The corporatism of the welfare state, its top-down policies and their implementation, the reliance on technical fixes and social management have increasingly been perceived with hostility by many recipients — women, Afro-Caribbean and Asian people, the unemployed, the young. The impenetrability of local and national government bodies and public service organisations encourages hostility, passivity, apathy. While means do exist to enable public scrutiny and intervention few people assume they have the right to participate and many would have to think twice about *how* they could. In the National Health Service no positions are elected at any level and there is no direct democracy at all.

Shake Up and Shape Up — A New Vision

It is clear then that traditional views of the welfare state have been shaken and that the gap between the public's rights to have needs met and the meeting of them is wide open. Thus in the face of attack, disillusionment, and the real weaknesses of the welfare state it is also clear that a politics of vision will be essential to defending what we still have and its transformation. For we shall need to invent a future that is desirable and in which full equality is made a reality — a popular future.

In terms of socially useful production it is important to recognise the value of services, but also the need for a re-evaluation of their content and purpose. For example, to make the leap from health care not just for the sick to be made fit for production, but for all to be fit for creative work and relations. Starting from this premise would suggest new links between different forms of public services.

Rather than hanging on to the abstraction of the public as a unity, a popular politics of social welfare would have to take on board the implications of a more differentiated view of social and individual needs that engages with the legitimate knowledge that people have of their own specific cultural and social circumstances and desires.

This in turn implies a new structure of social relations in which needs, aspirations, proposals and implementation could take place on the widest social basis as a process of critical evaluation and struggle. For a structure in which public participation is divorced from innovation and implementation weakens the potential social usefulness of provision for social need. A fully democratised structure of relations implies a combination of providers and users, a blurred distinction in any case, from which communities of interest could emerge and in which the political nature of the public services would be evident as a vital arena of political struggle. Which priorities are to be decided by whom? The expensive use of resources for heart transplants should be set against other needs such as geriatric care, and debated and decided democratically. A democratised structure will also mean examining the internal organisation of the welfare state where, for example, wasteful divisions of skill are maintained through hierarchy. In the NHS nursing skills are greater than the power to use them and doctors retain medical power themselves.

Ursula Huws noted that the skills of service are devalued as commonplace, and female, and argued that socially useful production too easily avoids the question of how a society cares for its members. This is partly to do with a recent history of struggles over the social use of technologies, which have not fully re-connected with earlier 19th Century struggles of the Utopian Socialists. Partly too with the patriarchal nature of British socialism. A modern Utopian Socialist vision will need to re-value the caring skills, re-distribute them between women and men, re-think 'productive' labour.

Inklings of a Future

It is possible to connect together events in different places that reflect some of the characteristics of a re-vitalised welfare state that we have been talking about. They are often smallscale and fragmentary but give an indication of the way ideas are forming.

Within the NHS struggles against hospital cuts and closures have drawn together hospital workers, management and patients and campaigns are developing over the qualitative aspects of healthcare. Community health-care and health education has begun to take on democratic forms in some places: inner city Birmingham for example. General Practice units in certain hospitals have existed for some years, providing a link between patient, family doctor and specialists in hospital. One (or perhaps more) GP practice has employed a nurse-practicioner who makes visits to patients, makes a diagnosis with them (rather than for them) and provides certain medication or treatments and only where necessary calls on the doctor. Arguably this is just a way of reducing costs and saving time, but also the influence of practices in third world countries is valuable. There Paramedics are trained to provide vital basic healthcare and education to large numbers of people often widely dispersed, with few medical resources and doctors. There are signs that hospital staff and GPs are beginning to recognise the cultural dimensions of medical care, like the distinct social customs, technologies and medical practices surrounding the management of health of ethnic communities now living in Britain. Signs too that these communities themselves are making their own particular demands of health and welfare provision.

Well-women clinics are being established both in and out of the NHS. Their starting points are that well-being is more than physical health, that it is also to do with social, economic, spiritual and emotional factors, and that purposeful activity is essential to maintaining passion and energy for life. Knowledge, control and care of our own bodies is necessary to accomplish well-being and in large measure people can and should act for themselves. Well-women clinics acknowledge the specific needs of women as women in particular economic, social and cultural circumstances.

There are things to be learned from places elsewhere. In Holland for example there is a far higher proportion of home confinements for first and subsequent births than here. The value of home confinement is that the level of technical intervention is reduced except for real necessity; mothers, fathers and other children experience less disruption to household routine and are involved in the birth; and the caring environment of the home, neighbours and friends can better support the mother. The use of valuable hospital beds and equipment is conserved for other needs, and childbirth is returned to the normal event it has been in the past. In Holland and the United States the midwives movement is of interest because they have re-claimed some control from the doctors.

Moving beyond the framework of a socially useful health service to another dimension in which socially useful production can be imagined it is worth noting the Miners' Strike of 1984-85. Although SUP did not exist as a political discourse within the struggle it was clearly there, as a historical undercurrent and within the ideas in currency. Clearly the strike was about useful work, a useful commodity and community viability. However, the politics of the struggle went well beyond this.

Coventry Mine, at Kersley a few miles outside Coventry is an isolated North Warwickshire mining community. Active in the strike it formed, as elsewhere, a women's support group, did its fair share of picketing inside and outside the area and set up community facilities like other places. As the strike progressed however the political ground and demands shifted — improvements in the local primary school were called for, there was talk of a community organised bus service. To sustain and retain the community forged in struggle, the notion of cooperatives was debated (partly because of knowledge gained via working relations established with a housing co-op in the city). History will show the final outcome of all this. There is nothing special about Kersley and for this reason the fertility of SUP as idea and politics is evident even though it was not formally introduced. What if it had been a fully fledged oppositional idea?

Final Thoughts

In many ways we are still looking at a very underdeveloped SUP politics, at the moment locked largely into reformism. SUP has been mythologised well beyond its concrete results. It has to be taken apart as a token. It should not be viewed or treated as a generality. The questions of socially useful to *whom* and *for what* and *under what conditions* have to be retained and answered at specific moments and sites of struggle. Likewise need has to be understood more fully and not reduced to utility.

Vulnerability to Left scientism should also be guarded against. The hidden hand of the Left technical expert can cast its own shadow. The socialist project must exceed the mechanics of technologies of power and recognise the full scope of the character of social need and human possibility. SUP then can and must be seen as a democratic process, rather than part of a technocratic vanguard. SUP has to be shifted outside the confines of the 'informed' sections of the radical movements into the arena of a broad political culture, becoming the focus of popular demands. We must have vivid, convincing ways of imagining what it would be.

However we should not underestimate that one of the great strengths of SUP is that it opens up the possibility of new political formations and alliances. This is vital at a time when the old ones are weakened. For example, in the most general terms, it can be viewed as a means to the strategic working together of red, green, peace, and feminist politics. Put another way the radical alternative to nuclear arms has to be a detailed conversion into peaceful projects. The conception and function of this project can however be of common interest to socialist futures. It can be ecologically sound, promote peace and be to the material advantage of women. What has to be developed with this, and all other examples, is a method and form to create the vision and represent it in such a way that it becomes politically attractive — demanded and desired.

The search for socially useful production is a challenge to activism. It engages the here and now. It threads through and across national boundaries and the forms of Left politics. It is the ground on which we may build new knowledges and experience, and create new kinds of action. It is the belief — we repeat — that social well-fare is productive labour, and productive labour a form of well-being.

Resources & Bibliography

Additional reading

Ackroyd, Margolis, Rosenhead, Shallilce. *The Technology of Political Control.* Pluto. 1981.
Anderson, P. *In the Tracks of Historical Materialism.* NLR/Verso. 1983.
Beckman, R. *Surviving the Second Great Depression.* Pan Books. 1983.
Braverman, R. *Labor, Monopoly and Capital.* Monthly Review Press, USA. 1974.
BSSRS. *Nuclear Power: The Rigged Debate.* 60p + p&p.
CAITS. *Workers' Plans: Cutting Edge or Slippery Slope.* 1980. £2.25.
Coates, K. ed. *The Right to Useful Work.* Spokesman. Nottingham. 1978.
Coventry, Liverpool, Newcastle & N. Tyneside Trades Councils. *State Intervention in Industry: A Workers' Inquiry,* second updated edition, Spokesman, 1982.
Dickson, D. *Alternative Technology and the Politics of Change.* Fontana. 1974.
Ehrenreich, B. and English, D. *Complaints and Disorders the Sexual Politics of Sickness.* Readers and Writers. 1976.
The Alternative Economic Strategy. A response by the Labour Movement to the economic crisis.
GLC (Greater London Council). *Jobs for a Change.* 90p.
GLC *London Industrial Strategy.* £5.
Gorz, A. *Farewell to the Working Class.* Penguin. 1983.
Gorz, A. *The Division of Labour: Labour Process and Class Struggle in Modern Capitalism.* Hassocks. Harvester Press. 1976.
Hastings, S. & Levie, H. *Privatisation?* Spokesman, 1983.
Hayden, D. *The Grand Domestic Revolution: A history of feminist designs for American homes, neighbourhoods and cities.* MIT Press. 1981.
Hebdige, D. *Subculture and the Meaning of Style.* Methuen. 1979.
Hill, C. *The World Turned Upside Down.* Penguin. 1975.
Huws, U. *The New Homeworkers.* Low Pay Unit. 1984. £2.50.
Huws, U. *Your Job in the '80s: A woman's guide to new technology.* Pluto. 1982.
Job Sharing and Job Splitting. Information from New Ways to Work. Available from 347a Upper Street, London N1. 60p.

Kropotkin, P. *Fields, Factories and Workshops Tomorrow.* George, Allen and Unwin. 1974.
Levie, H., Gregory, D. & Lorentzen, N. *Fighting Closures: De-industrialisation and the Trade Unions 1979-1983.* Spokesman, 1984.
Lineman, M. and Tucker, V. *Workers' Co-operatives: Potential and Problems.* University College Cork Bank of Ireland Centre for Co-operative Studies.
Loney, M. *Community Against Government: The British Community Development Projects 1968-78.* Heinemann. 1983.
Lucas Aerospace Confederation Trade Union Committee. *Lucas Aerospace.* 1979.
Morton, A.L. ed. *Political Writings of William Morris.* Lawrence and Wishart. 1973.
Noble, D. *America by Design.* Knopf, USA. 1977.
Ryle, M. *The Politics of Nuclear Disarmament.* Pluto. 1981.
Speke Joint Shop Stewards Committee. Dunlop: *Jobs for Merseyside.* CAITS. 1979.
Technology Policy Group. *Trade Union Policy and Nuclear Power.* Open University. 1981.
Third World Press. *Worldwatch Paper No.25. Worker Participation and the Quality of Work.* £1.25.
Whitfield, D. *Privatisation.* Pluto. 1983.
Yoxen, E. *The Gene Business.* Crucible Science or Society Series. Pan Books and Channel 4 TV. 1983.

Useful Addresses

1. Health

Disability Alliance, 21 Star Street, London W2 1QB. 01-402 7026.
Health Education Council, 78 New Oxford Street, London WC1. 01-637 1881.
Socialist Health Association, 9 Poland Street, WC1V 3DG.

2. Local, Central and Euro Government Agencies

Commission for Racial Equality (CRE), Elliot House, 10-12 Allington Street, London SW1E 5EF. 01-828 7022.
Equal Opportunities Commission (EOC), Overseas House, Quay Street, Manchester M3 3HN.
European Social Fund (ESF), Department of Employment, Overseas Division, Caxton House, Tothill Road, London SW1H 9NA. 01-213 3810/7623/5924/4305.

3. Nuclear Disarmament, Ecology, Science

Anti-Nuclear Campaign (ANC), PO Box 216, Sheffield 1. 0742-754691.
Bertrand Russell Peace Foundation, Gamble Street, Nottingham NG7 4ET, also *ENDpapers.*
British Society for Social Responsibility in Science (BSSRS), 9 Poland Street, London WC1V 3DG.

Campaign for Nuclear Disarmament (CND), 11 Goodwin Street, London N4 3HQ. 01-263 0977, also *Sanity* magazine.
European Nuclear Disarmament (END), Southbank House, Black Prince Road, London SE 17, also *END Journal*.
Friends of the Earth (FOE), 377 City Road, London EC1V 1NA. 01-837 0731.
Greenpeace Limited, Graham Street, London N1. 01-251 3020.
Medical Campaign Against Nuclear Weapons, 23a Tenison Road, Cambridge CB1 2DG. 0223-313828.
Socialist Environment and Resources Association (SERA), 9 Poland Street, London W1V 3DG.
World Information Service on Energy (WISE), 34 Cowley Road, Oxford. 0865-725354.

4. Technology

Centre for Alternative Industrial and Technological System (CAITS), Polytechnic of North London, Holloway Road, London N7. 01-607 7079.
Centre for Alternative Technology, Llwyngwern Quarry, Machynlleth, Powys. 0654 2400/2782.
Intermediate Technology Development Group, 9 King Street, Covent Garden, London WC2E 8HN. 01-836 9434.
Network for Alternative Technology and Technology Assessment (NATTA), c/o ATG, Faculty of Technology, Open University, Milton Keynes, Bucks.
Technology Policy Unit, University of Aston in Birmingham, Gosta Green, Birmingham 4. 021-359 3611.
Unit for the Development of Alternative Products (UDAP), Lanchester Polytechnic, Coventry CV1. 0203-24166 x.508.

Social Policy, Research, Campaigns

Campaign for Press and Broadcasting Freedom, 9 Poland Street, WC1V 3DG.
Conference of Socialist Economists (CSE), 25 Horsell Road, London N5 1XL. 01-607 9615, also *Capital and Class* magazine.
Counter Information Services (CIS), 9 Poland Street, WC1V 3DG.
Ethnic Minority Advice Project, 139 Spital Hall, Sheffield S4. 0742-754340.
Joint Docklands Action Group (J-DAG), 2 Cable Street, London E1 8JG. 01-480 5324.
Labour Research Department, 78 Blackfriars Road, London SE1 8HE. 01-928 3649.
Social Audit, 9 Poland Street, WC1V 3DG.
State Research, 9 Poland Street, WC1V 3DG.
Women's Research and Resources Centre (WRRC), 190 Upper Street, London N1. 01-359 5773.

Work

Industrial Common Ownership Movement (ICOM), 7/8 Corn Exchange, Leeds LS1 7BP. 0532-461737, and ICOM London — 7 Bradbury Street, London N16 8JN. 01-249 2837.
Immigrants Employment Rights Unit, 439 Harrow Road, London W10. 01-960 5746.
Institute of Workers' Control, Bertrand Russell House, Gamble Street, Nottingham NG7 4ET. 0602-784504.
Low Pay Unit, 9 Poland Street, London W1. 01-437 1780.
Co-operative Development Agency (national), 20 Albert Embankment, London SE1 7TJ. 01-211 4633.
Network of Labour and Community Research and Resource Centres, c/o Leeds TUCRIC, 6 Blenheim Terrace, Leeds 2. 0532-39633.
Right to Work Campaign, c/o 265a Seven Sisters Road, London N4 2DE.
Unemployment Centres, c/o your local Citizen's Advice Bureau, Regional TUC, or Trades Union Congress, Congress House, Gt Russell Street, London WC1B 3LS. 01-636 4030.

Exhibition

There is an exhibition available which takes up the key theme of this book — social usefulness. It explores different ways in which we can recognise and understand need. Planned to coincide with the publication and can be used in conjunction with the book, it is also intended that the exhibition can have an independent existence.

As with the book this exhibition attempts to pose the need to develop ways of representing socially useful production that can engage in productive debate and activity.

The exhibition is appropriate for many purposes since it can be used both as introduction to the issues and for specific purpose in education, work, TU, community, local government, peace, women's and other cultural groupings.

Further details and booking arrangements can be made through us at: Collective Design/Projects, 2 Station Road, King's Heath, Birmingham B14 7SR. Tel: 021 443 5232.

We should also welcome responses to this book. We have plans for further related projects and would be glad of comments and contacts (at the above address).

Contributors

Cliff Alum and Vin McCabe share wide experience in the labour movement and are founding worker members of the Coventry Trades Council Unemployed Workers Project.

Erica Carter is a comparative researcher on Britain and West Germany. Founding member of Material Word, a Birmingham-based translation agency specialising in academic texts.

Cynthia Cockburn is a researcher. She is the author of *The Local State*, a study of welfare services in a London borough, and of *Brothers*, an account of male trade unionists' responses to technological and social change in the printing industry.

Philip Cooke is a lecturer in Planning Theory and Urban Politics at UWIST, Cardiff. He is a member of the editorial board of *Radical Wales*, and has research interests in theories of development in peripheral regions and state intervention in urban problems.

Mike Cooley was prominent in the Lucas Combine Shop Stewards' Committee. He is the author of *Architect or Bee?*, a book about human labour processes. He joined the Greater London Enterprise Board with responsibility for new technology networks.

Paul Field is a long-standing member of Coventry Workshop and active in the Coventry left and community politics.

Ursula Huws is a researcher. She is the author of *Your Job in the '80s* and of *Homeworkers*, a study for the Low Pay Unit.

Chris Lee is a former overseas worker and early member of Third World Publications.

Sonia Liff currently works at the Technology Policy Unit, University of Aston. She recently completed a doctoral thesis on the sexual and technological division of labour.

John Lovering works at the Centre for Regional and Urban Research, University of Bristol. He has published a number of articles on the political economy of Wales, including *Gwynedd – A County in Crisis*, Coleg Harlech Occasional Papers in Welsh Studies, No 2.

Seymour Melman teaches at Columbia University, New York. He is the author of *Pentagon Capitalism* and of many other studies, and an early contributor to the arms conversion debate.

David Noble teaches at the Smithsonian Institution, Washington DC. He is the author of *America by Design*, an account of the relation between scientific and technical education and the labour process.

Dave Pelly works for the Centre for Alternative Industrial and Technological Systems (CAITS), London. He is a frequent writer on arms control issues.

Hilary Wainwright writes on socialist and feminist issues. She is co-author of *Beyond the Fragments* and of *The Lucas Plan*, and has joined the GLC's Popular Planning Unit.

PRIVATISATION?

edited by: Sue Hastings and Hugo Levie

THE AIM of this important study is to give a blow-by-blow account of the Tories' extensive programme of privatisation and the responses that so far seem most successful. This volume will be of particular interest to public sector trade unionists who are faced with privatisation, because it helps to set some key special cases in the wider context of the Conservative attack on all public services and utilities. Examples range from the NHS and National Freight Corporation, via the gas showrooms, direct labour organisations and refuse collection to British Telecom and the Civil Service.

Privatisation? calls upon all those convinced of the need to defend the public sector to stop and think. What have we done wrong in the past, that leads so many people to be confused about the importance of an expanding instead of a shrinking public sector?

Contributing unions include:

- COHSE
- NALGO
- NUPE
- POEU
- SCPS
- TGWU
- UCATT

"This book will be of practical value to workers and trade union representatives fighting to keep valuable services public".
Rodney K. Bickerstaffe,
General Secretary, NUPE.

". . . by far the most informative account yet available of the process of privatisation".
Public Money

205pp, Illustrated, £15 & £4.95

SPOKESMAN
Bertrand Russell House, Gamble Street, Nottingham NG7 4ET
0602 708318

RIGHT TO A HOME
Labour Housing Group

Right to a Home offers a radical blueprint for Labour's future housing policies. Written by socialists active in the Labour Housing Group, it argues that the Labour Party must effectively challenge the Tories' appalling record on housing by advancing an imaginative alternative vision.

Starting from the principle of the right to a home for all members of the community, the Labour Housing Group spells out a fresh approach to a collection of tangled problems: funding for council and owner occupied housing; discrimination against women; housing and race; private landlords; design and standards and housing renewal. Encouragement for housing co-ops and the roles for housing associations come under the spotlight. There are also concise and reliable briefings on reforming housing finance and investment.

Right to a Home will be of interest to all those seeking more choice in housing, the opportunity for greater control over their own homes, and a housing policy that is just and fair.

Contributors:

- Marion Brion
- Tim Daniel
- Jane Darke
- Christine Davies
- Mike Gibson
- David Griffiths
- Steve Hilditch
- Chris Holmes
- Bernard Kilroy
- Stewart Lansley
- Richard Moseley
- John Perry
- Bert Provan
- Geoff Randall
- Nick Raynsford
- Alan Simpson
- Selwyn Ward
- Tristan Wood

LABOUR HOUSING GROUP exists to promote discussion of housing issues within the Labour movement and to campaign locally and nationally for the implementation of socialist housing policies.

194pp, £15 & £4.95
SPOKESMAN
Bertrand Russell House, Gamble Street, Nottingham NG7 4ET
0602 708318